CONVERSATIONS WITH AUDEN

Howard Griffin

CONVERSATIONS WITH AUDEN

Edited by Donald Allen

Grey Fox Press
San Francisco

The publication of this book was partially supported by a grant from the National Endowment for the Arts, Washington, D.C., a federal agency.

Front cover photograph of W. H. Auden in 1949 by George Platt Lynes.

Library of Congress Cataloging in Publication Data

Griffin, Howard, 1915–1975.
  Conversations with Auden.

  Includes index.
  1. Auden, Wystan Hugh, 1907–1973—Interviews.
2. Poets, English—20th century—Interviews. I. Auden, Wystan Hugh, 1907–1973. II. Title.
PS3501.U55Z68   1981   821'.912   80-24381
ISBN 0-912516-55-0
ISBN 0-912516-56-9 (pbk.)

Distributed by The Subterranean Company,
P.O. Box 10233, Eugene, Oregon 97440.

Contents

Editor's note

In the fall of 1946 Howard Griffin wrote Wystan Hugh Auden offering his services as a secretary. Auden replied: "Thank you very much for your letter and kind offer. I could not, of course, dream of letting you work gratis, but I do often have little jobs of one sort and another where I need secretarial help, for which I would pay whatever the standard rates are. If you are free, could you come here Tuesday at about 5.00 p.m. and we could talk it over."

Griffin was then thirty-one. He had grown up in the Westbury area of Long Island, the son of a prosperous farm-supply family, and he had attended Columbia University for a time. During the forties he had edited a Long Island news-paper, then worked as a secretary in Manhattan, and pub-lished his poems and stories in leading literary magazines. His first book of poems, *Cry Cadence*, would be published the following year by Farrar, Straus. He was of course fasci-nated by Auden, whom he much admired; throughout his life he had an intense curious interest in people he liked. The diaries he kept faithfully year after year are said to be filled with details of his encounters with painters and writers, all meticulously recorded in a combination of shorthand and private code.

Auden, then thirty-nine, had won considerable fame as poet, librettist, essayist and lecturer, both in his native England and in the United States where he had emigrated in 1939, becoming a citizen in 1945. He had published some dozen volumes of poems and plays and accounts of travels to China and Iceland. *The Age of Anxiety*, a long poem he had been working on since 1944, was published in 1947; it won a Pulitzer prize and established Auden as *the* poet of that very difficult age.

In the late forties Auden was renting apartment 4E at 7 Cornelia Street, in New York's Greenwich Village. In these "unbelievably untidy" quarters the conversations took place from time to time over the next several years when Auden and Griffin were both in the city. They clearly reflect Auden's interests and often echo his writings of that period. For instance, during the 1946–1947 term he lectured on Shakespeare at the New School, traversing all thirty-seven plays in their supposed chronological order.

The conversations are not verbatim transcriptions of actual talk. This was before the common use of tape recorders, and in any case, Auden would not have permitted the intrusion of such an instrument. Griffin must have made elaborate notes of their talks in shorthand and then later typed them out, gradually reworking his material to achieve the effect he wanted. No doubt he had in mind the famous example of Johann Peter Eckermann's *Conversations with Goethe in the Later Years of His Life*. Here, too, the more famous writer is given the best lines, and the interlocutor plays the lesser role of planning the talks, keeping the conversation flowing, and then later shaping and polishing the dialogues until he has achieved the desired perfection of form. In other words, Griffin was not conducting the ordinary interview we now daily encounter, often completely innocent of any editorial attention, in all the media; he was attempting a literary form with its own inherent interest and validity. In May of 1949, Auden wrote him from Ischia: "Many thanks for your letter and the dialogue. I don't remember saying a word which you attribute to me, but I seem to agree with what you say, so it must be alright. I hope *Politics* pays you."

Dwight Macdonald's *Politics* did not publish the dialogue it was offered, but Griffin was able to place all eight with other magazines: *Accent* published the first in 1949, the fourth in 1952 and the seventh in 1953. *Hudson Review* published the second in 1951, *Poetry* a much abbreviated version of the third in 1953, *Partisan Review* the sixth, and *Semi-colon* the eighth in the same year. The fifth was included in *The Avon Book of Modern Writing*, an anthology Philip Rahv edited in 1953.

The conversations were highly regarded in literary circles in the fifties. Marianne Moore, for example, wrote Griffin in 1953 that she found "these discussions . . . profitable to me if no one else"; and she added: "The unfalsified diction and directness are what are assets in these equivocal times! (A model of the 'un-messy.')"

I knew the extremely shy and diffident poet Howard Griffin a little then. His poems I had read and the dialogues as they appeared in the literary magazines. We had met, probably in 1951, and now and then we got together for a lengthy argument over dinner, usually at the San Remo, on such burning issues as the 1949 Kinsey report on *Sexual Behavior in the Human Male*—he was unflinchingly and perversely, from my point of view, opposed to it.

When he came to look for a publisher for his conversations with Auden he naturally thought of the young Grove Press, where I was working as an editor. Both Barney Rosset and I found his project intriguing and valuable, but in the end, and after considerable discussion, we agreed in doubting that the book would have enough appeal for the general reading public to justify the costs of production. This was at the beginning of the rise of the quality paperback which was soon to revolutionize American trade book publishing.

No doubt Griffin offered his book to other possible publishers, with much the same response. When he died in 1975, two years after Auden's death, also in Austria, the work for which he was best known had still not found publication in book form. It was only a few years later that Nell Blaine recalled my earlier interest in the conversations and offered me a second chance to undertake their publication.

I am deeply indebted to Nell Blaine, executrix of the estate of Howard Griffin, for her generous assistance in preparing the conversations for publication. Grateful acknowledgment is also made to Edward Mendelson, literary executor of the estate of W. H. Auden, and to the editors who first published the dialogues: Kerker Quinn, Frederick Morgan, Karl Shapiro, William Phillips, Philip Rahv, and John Bernard

Myers. Charles Osborne's *W. H. Auden: The Life of a Poet* (Harcourt, 1979) and Alonzo Gibbs' "The Kinsman Affair," *Long Island Forum*, October 1976, have been valuable aids in the composition of this note. W. H. Auden's and Marianne Moore's letters to Howard Griffin in the Henry W. and Albert A. Berg Collection of the New York Public Library, are quoted here with the permission of Edward Mendelson, Executor of the Estate of W. H. Auden, and that of the Library. I owe a debt of gratitude to Valerie Estes for her study of the text, to William Turner for his patient work in designing the book, and to John Geddes for his careful reading of the proofs.

D.A., May 1981

Howard Griffin: A Personal Note

I first met Howard Griffin at a party at Jane Freilicher's in 1954, the same party that Howard describes as his first meeting with Frank O'Hara, in a 1966 journal. The Dialogs with Auden had caused a respectable stir, and as a painter vitally involved with various poets of intersecting circles, I was quite aware of Howard's achievements and considerable reputation at that time. He belonged, as a younger member and later appendage, to that illustrious group of English poets and intellectuals referred to in *The Children of the Sun,* which included Isherwood, Auden, Spender and Kinross—as well as to his contemporaries of the New York School. Lord Kinross made Howard a leading character in his book *Innocents at Home.* Despite these wide literary associations and a gift for making new acquaintances, he remained essentially a lonely, shy man and a figure, even then, of considerable mystery.

Like many artists, he shared an aversion to psychoanalysis and viewed surveys with mistrust. This mistrust extended to most literary critics and to literary establishment tastes. Many of his true beliefs were hidden behind a wry humor and an interviewer's contrariness—a skillful technique for getting a rise out of his subject.

After an inheritance in 1963, his efforts to publish were intermittent. He bought a fine old country house on the Dorset coast, and later in 1969 he acquired an alpine farmhouse in the Tirol at the opposite end of Austria from Auden! Despite these domestic leanings, he still spent a lot of time traveling. One home away from homes was a lonely medieval tower on the coast of Sicily.

His friendship with Auden lasted twenty-seven years, and in the summer of 1975, he writes that he poured a libation of brandy on Auden's grave at Kirchstetten.

Although his great respect for Auden remained constant

until his own death at sixty, Howard's work took a very different and independent direction. His poetry achieved a touching personal tone and earthy simplicity. Most of his later works remain to be published, with his place in literature yet to be established.

Nell Blaine

CONVERSATIONS WITH AUDEN

one

Howard Griffin: Would you rather have lived at an earlier time when men knew less, when there was no police force, no plumbing?

W. H. Auden: I would not. If one thinks in terms of happiness or love, human behavior certainly has not improved through the ages, but if one thinks in terms of knowledge, power and potential for good, one must say: there has been an advance.

Griffin: You mean at least we have technological advantages?

Auden: Yes. The power instruments. You cannot have advances in science without having the good and bad, without being given a choice. It is always up to men to decide how they are going to use what they have. With each new invention, the question of free will is resurrected. The first invention of all was the apple—divine knowledge which caused the trouble. The story of Chapters 2 and 3 of Genesis is a myth to explain history. One must acknowledge its poetic truth, for human beings still seem much like Adam and Eve, blaming things on each other, and desiring to be gods. Out of their monstrous vanity human creatures want to be their own cause. Adam succumbed to the temptation to eat the apple—but not out of appetite.... The story of the Fall has to be told in mythical terms because it is what conditions history. In Genesis we do not have a race of people but the first man and woman, and the first thing they do is eat of the tree, an act that begins time and loses them this innocence. Civilization in itself remains neutral and ambiguous. All forms of knowledge and power

1

have two sides. As temptations, they can make a man behave either much better or much worse.

Griffin: You make it quite clear that knowledge, though it can make one more responsible, say, or more conscious, cannot make one choose good or reject evil.

Auden: Yes, it seems to me that a man learns to choose the good by desiring it. By sincerely wishing to be good, a reciprocity is set up between act and intent, metaphorically similar to the mirrors in the *Paradiso*.

Griffin: In this ethical realm, does the artist have an advantage?

Auden: Although the practice of an art can make a man more human perhaps, it has no power to change malice into virtue. For all art is the production of an artifact, a thing, an act often performed more ably by the laborer. Since he is a narcissist, the artist loves to play a part. Conceivably he may find himself in the role of a villain and be fascinated by the spectacle of himself in this guise. You may ask how one goes about changing... well...

Griffin: Yes. It is hard to say just what I mean. Rilke closed his poem "Archaic Torso of Apollo" with "For there is no place that does not see you. You must change your life." In other words he seemed to believe that a profound aesthetic experience could cause a man to really change and rededicate his life.

Auden: Although aesthetic powers give one pleasure, they do not make one good. How does one change?... One can look ahead, one can say: I *should do* this. Will I do it? A part of the mind looks on; a part decides. Also, one must not discount Grace.

Griffin: You mean supernatural intervention—the light that appeared to Saul on the road to Damascus?

Auden: Not really supernatural, at least not in the sense of miraculous. It may be perfectly natural. It depends on an intensification of normal powers of sensitivity and contemplation. Matthew was lured from the ballot box by a word of

2

Christ's but only because the command was spoken in a certain way to the right man. True enough, at a particular time Augustine heard the boy chanting *"tolle legge, tolle legge"* and in his sorrow became converted to Christianity; but before that, we must remember, a long period of hesitation and psychological unrest occurred. Oftentimes these ethical changes are not as clear-cut as commentators would have us believe. All we know is: at one point something pushes people over the edge and in these changes suffering plays a greater part than knowledge. The metamorphosis often occurs in the early thirties. You agree, don't you, that any kind of theological persuasion plays no role in these moral changes?

Griffin: I believe that usually comes later—a post-intellectualization of belief.

Auden *(taking a book down from a shelf)*: Caesarius has some wonderful things to say about this. Listen . . . "Some seem to be converted by the direct call and inspiration of God, others by nothing but an instigation from the spirit of evil, some by a certain levity of mind but the greatest number are converted by the ministry of others, as by the word of exhortation, the power of prayer or the effect of example. A vast number are drawn to the order by different exigencies, such as sickness or poverty, or reaction from danger, or by the terror of hell, or by the longing for the heavenly country. . . ."

Griffin: Yes, the "longing for the heavenly country." I believe that the idea of a more perfect state exists as a pattern of human consciousness, not merely as an eschatologic assumption.

Auden: The Garden of Eden idea serves to remind human beings that they are fallible and have to be redeemed. All men are erring; consequently one would not put any man in office unconditionally; all tenures and cumulative wages would be checked. To say that men are sometimes converted because of a "longing for the heavenly country" may mean (1) that they conceive of a monastic life as a "soft escape," (2) that the idea of a lost happiness really forms part of their thought. In eighteenth-century romantic landscape art, one finds a manifestation of this. Within a huge natural setting, the human figure is dwarfed, but the effect is not one of real terror, but a kind of delicious shock. In this school nature is portrayed as friendly, clean, clear, etc. without bugs, snakes and prefabricated houses. Rousseau's cosmology is a version of the Golden Age. Another aspect of it is the view of D. H. Lawrence, who draws a contrast between the reflective mental consciousness and the dark gods of the blood. We can see the feelings that would bring this about: in an industrial civilization we live a certain type of life. During our summer vacations we visit a community of simple people whose degree of self-consciousness (as distinguished from belief) is not very great. We observe that they are happier than we are; that they behave better.... One should contrast this idea of an idyllic primitiveness with the school to which Lucretius, Vergil and Hobbes belonged that conceived of the original state of man as savage, and posited civilization as the metamorphosis of the brutal and ignorant into an ordered, civil world, a change that was brought about, according to the myths, by Hercules, Prometheus and Tubal Cain.

Griffin: What is the danger of the Golden Age view?

Auden: It leads not to conservatism, but to a kind of nihilism. A we-are-all-sunk feeling; one had better withdraw. The withdrawal can take various forms: the attempt to live in a simpler manner or the way-out drinking or any other means to reduce self-consciousness.... Surely it is very easy for the Marxist to point out that this view has a natural appeal to a person who himself belongs to a dying class. On the other hand, the Hobbesian picture appeals to people who like power either of the reactionary or the forward-looking kind. Since they posit primitivism as a time of disorder, they put the Golden Age not at the beginning

4

but at the other end and they relate themselves causally to the achievement of this millennium. The Church describes the world starting out with the Garden, declining and progressing finally to the City of God. The danger lies in the probability that the institution will consider itself causally and by its nature related to the Divine City. The free, non-aristocratic view believes in the weakness and perfectibility of man divorced from the monist approach that progress will be accomplished by means of any political or religious device.

Griffin: Do you think a pessimistic view of human nature necessitates a strictly stratified society?

Auden: No. A certain amount of distinction between classes may be good. Only those should rule who are capable of ruling. In society there are places for benevolent rule and for submission but the submission should be sincere and the rule honest. Ideally in a democracy anyone can get to the top and rule but this, of course, does not work out in practice. Actually the democratic system means that everyone is managed by particularly endowed persons. It is more like what Steffens called "A government of the people by gentlemen for the businessmen."

Griffin: When we started out, I assumed we would get around to the question of free will. From remarks you made earlier, I assume you disagree with the priestly interpretation of the Fall as a symbol of the birth of morality.

Auden: Yes, I see it as a symbol of the human desire to be free, to be autonomous.

Griffin: I would like to go into this. You compared the temptation of the apple to the temptation of power-media, pointing out that, far from being curses or bogies, these essentially neutral objects may be presented to us repeatedly in many guises to cause us, wayward as we are, to make a right choice. If this is so, it is the mechanics of the choice which bothers me.

Auden: Choosing is an extremely rare phenomenon.

Human beings think they choose when, oftentimes, they obey an instinct, act gratuitously, or follow the suggestions of others. Seldom, for instance, does a man determine his lifework; it determines him. The most difficult thing for a man to succeed in doing is what he has a real talent for. And although the cliché of the fairy tale is: The prince *chose* his wife, in real life no one chooses a wife, as the wife knows.

Griffin: What happens when an individual loses the power to make a real decision between two alternatives?

Auden: He becomes a member of the crowd. If one asks why he cannot choose, one must say that a person in order to choose must believe in aesthetic values in terms of which a choice becomes meaningful. If persons cannot choose between rival loves, they cannot form a community. This has nothing to do with education, because knowing a lot does not make one believe in anything. Collectively knowing a lot does not give people a real function in society.

Griffin: Why did you say in the [*Portable Greek*] *Reader*, "The weakest point in Greek ethics is the analysis of Choice."

Auden: When human creatures and the world are new, they do not desire what they consider the restriction of choice, not seeing beyond the idea of pleasure. The function of youth is to go everywhere, do everything. In the early Greek myths almost all choices are made between essentially material objects: Paris must choose between the control of Asia, power in war and a pretty wife. In order for this to involve a real decision, these things are rightly equated. Marpessa must choose between Apollo and Idas, between two types of pleasure. Parallelly, Ulysses must choose between Calypso and Penelope, and he makes essentially the same choice as Marpessa. Penelope must choose between her father and husband, between two symbols of authority, but with the Christian era we get away from these easy choices, which are merely the hesitation between two enjoyments. Christ and St. Paul taught people that one might, one sometimes *should*, desire the physically disadvantageous

6

that, in other words, one might choose out of spite or defiance. In a world-scheme that posited pain and endurance as values, one might choose suffering. Realistically—although not gratuitously—Christ *chose* to be delivered to the priests and be killed (as we see in Chapter 20 of Matthew). In the first century A.D. it begins to appear that to choose, with a deliberate exercise of the will rather than reason, contumely, defeat and renunciation may be a kind of success. Therefore what Dostoyevsky called the "most advantageous advantage" might be, really, loss and exclusion.

Griffin: Someone has said that, though men live most of their lives at the will of others, it always remains within their power to choose their deaths, and thus to exercise autonomy. According to this, the most personal act a man can commit is his own death.

Auden: Yes, but not the deaths of others. That remains pretty impersonal. . . .We use the insectile word "extermination" to describe it.

Griffin: There seemed to be great gratuitousness about the mass killings of the Jews. Hitler had to keep his men occupied. It appeared to be a decision made out of frivolity; a question of: What shall we do next? Let's kill the Jews.

Auden: Although he seemed to be always telling other people what to do, Hitler's acts were determined by compulsion and desire for prestige. Men like Hitler, Napoleon and Richard III contrive to make their surroundings sufficiently exciting so that they are sustained in a *state of passion*, which dictates what they will do. People like Hitler have a hunger for complete mastery and when things begin to go wrong, then there is nothing for them to do but wish their death. The Hitler type is able to choose for others, but incapable of self-choice and he must go on arousing enemies because their fact proves that he exists. When we read of the night of the long knives, the SS slogan "Heads must roll," the Rohm purge, etc., we see that the Nazi leaders contrived to do evil consciously for its own sake in order to demonstrate their objective reality. They were demonics.

Griffin: How do you define a demonic character?

Auden: A demonic character is one who is impelled into action for the sake of action. He is rash, irresponsible—not mischievous, for that implies malice whereas a demonic may set out with the intention to do good, to save a town, to win the day.

Griffin: Such a person as Joan of Arc?

Auden: Or Hitler. A person with a sense of fate, even a love of fate as strong-willed people often have. Once they get started they cannot stop. Their fatality is being what they are; they are their own disease.... Because circumstances impelled him into action, most of Hitler's acts cannot be explained logically.... The extermination of the Jews, the mass murder of children, killing to music. Essentially the Nazis were bored. Ennui causes people to take a leap into action. Distrusting words, believing in deeds, the Hitler type uses language as an actor, that is, to deceive. By language he makes people want what he wants them to want. At first, he seems to have great success; others succumb to him....

Griffin: And this is the moment of great danger, isn't it, the moment of infatuation?

Auden: Yes... For the dictator, war is a good thing; then he feels wanted. He has a hunger to be needed. A war provides people with a negative sense of self—enough self to destroy. What Hitler, Napoleon and Alexander lacked was a consciousness of their finiteness, a lack that can be disastrous. Many leaders of history, revered by their people, are moved by criminal folly and are guilty.

Griffin: I think of Byron's reference to Wellington: "You are the best of cutthroats...."

Auden: Wellington was just an opportunist. It is difficult to find demonics among the English... too lymphatic... Achilles is a demonic: Odysseus, an opportunist. In advance

8

Achilles knew he would not return from the Trojan War. . . .
If a person knows his limitations (and, although the English
are conceited, they are not proud in the grand worldly way)
he cannot be a demonic.

Griffin: Roland is a demonic.

Auden: His rashness is a crime. When they are caught in
the rearguard action, Oliver wisely tells his friend to ask for
help, but Roland, thinking of the praise he will receive in
France, refuses. He will not blow the horn because of what
his parents might think of him. This is all very well but his
pride involves the deaths of others. A glory-hound. He
speaks of booty and urges his friend to battle. We see in the
Chanson that the relation of men in war is one of passion
united by fear. How does Roland confront death? In dying
he does not think of his fiancee but of his reputation and
conquest. Essentially renown in war is an ego satisfaction on
a level with success in business.

Griffin: In the old legends the hero claims invulnerabili-
ty except for one spot. Does this form a kind of revenge
against those who set themselves up as gods?

Auden: If a person claims to be immune, he is hiding
from himself the fact that he is human. *Hubris* involves over-
security whereas the basis of pride is lack of security, anxiety
and defiance. Only men of great power can be guilty of
hubris. The demonic believes that power comes from him
and this arouses the envy of the gods; for this he receives
punishment. Knowing he is not a god, he wills to make
himself one. Pride can be defined as a form of despair. The
lower form involves willing not to be oneself. The higher
form: not willing to be oneself.

Griffin: The Greeks restricted the sense of guilt. In other
words, the member of a Greek chorus could not suffer from
hubris.

Auden: Exactly. The Christian tradition defines pride as
a more general thing. In fact, no one is exempt. Pride is
something any of us—no matter what our position—may

suffer from. This view largely changes the role of fate which becomes less important than character, personal or social. A person with this view cannot be called a demonic. He is not in love with fate, neither does he fight fate. Accepting his finiteness, he takes the moment and what he makes of it depends on his decision.

Griffin: The demonic is he who embraces and fights with his fate as Jacob with the angel?

Auden: Yes.... One of the most wonderful of the cartoons in *The New Yorker* showed a little man struggling madly with a huge octopus issuing from a manhole. An utterly passive crowd surrounded him. On the fringe of the crowd two men—Charles Addams characters—were walking by, ignorant of the cause of the disturbance. One carried a folded umbrella that looked exactly like a magician's wand. He turned to the other with the remark "It doesn't take much to attract a crowd in New York." The individual struggling with fate is hemmed in by the crowd, some of whom say to themselves: Thank God, it isn't me. Others think: Nothing exciting ever happens to me! And the two men on the periphery assume that it doesn't take much to make people look; therefore they'll do the opposite; they'll solve the problem by not looking. How did the German people react to Hitler? Some thought: He is suffering for us. See how he suffers! Others thought: He is full of power. I envy him!—Whereas America and England turned away and refused to look. . . .

two

The room was large, filled with haphazard furniture and the twelve volumes of an unabridged Oxford dictionary. After fixing coffee, Auden began talking about the nature of propaganda during wartime. I mentioned that in the army I had been disturbed by the claim, made by Americans, that the Japanese killed their own wounded.

Auden: That is a practice always attributed to the other side. Propaganda, like the lying of children, is due to fear and boredom.

Griffin: But why is this considered good propaganda?

Auden: The reason that such statements have great psychological effect is that they change what was an abstract relation into a personal relation. In war the relation between killer and killed is not a personal relation: each sees in the other not a person but the surrogate for an enemy force, not necessarily an armed surrogate. Furthermore, if the enemy is *not seen* (as is most often the case in modern war), the possibility of any sense of personal relation is decreased. In murder there must be intention to kill and a personal relation. In the case of the killing of one's wounded a personal relation is created: these men are not distant representatives of an enemy force.

One must distinguish between this and the execution of war prisoners. In the case of the attempted suicide of the Japanese war minister, a relation was brought in on a peculiarly personal plane. I am thinking of General Tojo, who was saved from death by the donation of the blood of an American army sergeant. Science has introduced a new kind of relation that has profound mystical effect on civilians.

Griffin: How would you classify the Nuremberg Trials?

Auden: Inevitably a personal relation was introduced. The accused were allowed to express their wills. The war trials were unique because they created a new rapprochement between the killing in war which is impersonal and the execution of killers who have been personally convicted. . . . But to return to our starting point—the killing of one's wounded and of prisoners. The reason why the refusal of quarter arouses indignation among civilians is that the human will is directly involved. Why do people enjoy detective stories?

Griffin: Because there is a personal relation between killer and killed?

Auden: Exactly. In a detective story you must have a murder; no other crime will do. Unless it is a murder, you don't care to find out who did it. Why in a detective story does one want to discover the criminal?

Griffin: Perhaps because in other offenses the law acts on behalf of the injured party, but in a personal crime like murder the community becomes a substitute for the victim and you, as an individual part, feel involved.

Auden: Yes. Connected with this is the great need of people who murder to confess. How does one feel at the end of the story when the murderer is caught? It is not satisfactory if the murderer goes mad or commits suicide. If he goes mad, he cannot ask forgiveness: for this reason those who regarded the Nuremberg Trials as a blood feud felt cheated when Hess was let off. If the murderer commits suicide he refuses to be forgiven. An example of this: Lady Macbeth.

Griffin: And this was the reason many felt cheated when Goering outwitted his jailers?

Auden: Yes, they wanted the death in itself. I was glad when I heard about his suicide. It showed up the stupidity of the American officers. Even a lieutenant-colonel should know that an X-ray must be taken of a prisoner to see if he has poison hidden in his rectum.

Americans regarded the death of Hitler with feelings that are more properly aroused by the detective story or the epic poem.

Griffin: Yes, you see the detective part of it in Trevor-Roper's book. [*The Last Days of Hitler*, 1947.]

Auden: The Siegfried part comes out in the attitude of the people. Those who do not believe that Hitler really died look upon him as an epic hero of whom the legend is that he is not dead, that he will return to save his country. This belief survives in England in regard to King Arthur.

Griffin: According to your distinction between war and murder, I would infer that a war cannot be waged unless personal antagonism is built up on the emotional level, and on the actual plane the personal relation minimized?

Auden: That is right. There was much less hand to hand combat in this war than in the last. The distances of aerial warfare have introduced a new element. When bombs are dropped from a great height, the act of killing becomes an *acte gratuit*. One bomb may drop on an orphan asylum and kill two or three thousand children. A man would feel differently if he were ordered to machine-gun an equal number of children. There was considerable gratuitousness in the dropping of bombs—among the British particularly.

Griffin: But still the personal relation in the last war was not completely destroyed?

Auden: By no means. In occupied countries, for instance, it recurs. Although a nonfraternization policy tries to cope with troubles brought about by the contiguity of conquered and conqueror, the personal relation inevitably creeps in. . . . The occupied *have something* which the occupiers want—not only material things or sexual pleasure but good will. They have destroyed this, or tried to. Nevertheless they desire profoundly, perhaps unconsciously, to be forgiven. Conquered and conqueror know that restitution is impossible and yet—whether they know it or not—the conqueror desires to offer restitution. He is both an exile and a killer; he wants to be regarded as a human being.

Griffin: That is true.... When a prisoner of war escapes from confinement in an enemy country, an interesting situation occurs. Say such a person is pursued and seeks refuge in some house and is taken in.

Auden: It is interesting because such a story concerns the conflict between the personal and the political will.

Griffin: The film *Grand Illusion* beautifully illustrated this conflict. The French prisoner who has been separated from his outfit takes refuge in a German house. There is an episode where he begins to fall in love with the woman of the house, who he fears will betray him. Although they live together for a time happily, at the end he has not even learned to say *"blaue augen."* And when they part, she corrects his pronunciation.

Auden: In *The Merchant of Venice* you find another illustration. The society depicted here is quite democratic ... the people are free and the freedom involves the most enormous obligations on the part of those who love. Their feelings for their friends transcend all family, racial or national loyalties. These people would agree with E. M. Forster's remark: "If I had to choose between betraying my country and betraying my friend, I hope I'd have the guts to betray my country." I believe that what people really should aspire to is a beneficent anationality.

Griffin: Don't you think that patriotism and love of country are, for the most part, "home front sentiments"?

Auden: Oh yes, but one must distinguish between patriotism and love of one's native soil. It is only in small communities—such as the Greek republics or the Swiss cantons—where they coincide. A man's attachment to the soil must tend toward narrowness. It is the most fully developed nations who have outgrown this love of the soil for they have learned to be unafraid of the unknown. There resides in some men—perhaps latently in all—a social longing, a desire to join with other men to form associations. . . .

Griffin: In unofficial records of the war you find occasions when the personal relation negates the political. The sympathy of percussion. In terms of experience and general feeling, the soldier may feel he has more in common with the enemy soldier than with people back home. Instances occur when the personal breaks through: Christmas truces, cigarettes being flung across the lines, cease-fires to take care of the wounded, etc. Also, in stories concerning the first World War one found another situation which brought about personal understanding: one soldier is forced to confront a man he has fatally wounded and compelled to watch that man die. As he dies, the other sees him become, not the hated, but a human being.

Auden: The situation of Wilfred Owen's "Strange Meeting."

Griffin: The personal may be brought in through the younger generation, as you do with the boy and girl in *On the Frontier.*

Auden: But here another difficulty occurs—a difficulty not amenable to change, and that is: the divorce of understanding and experience between generations. From experience, the older generation has understanding. Whereas the younger generation has a desire for experience. The frivolity of art is that it cannot have much effect in changing people. No matter how utterly convincing, didactic art cannot succeed in changing society. The reason of men can be swayed, it is true, but men are essentially unreasonable. The best definition of man is the ungrateful biped. Men are ungrateful, mischievous; they are not—for the most part—artists or artisans.

Griffin: You mean art, like law, is always trying to catch up with life?

Auden: Yes, and vainly. A young person cannot be deterred from participating in war by reading a book such as

All Quiet [*on the Western Front*], say, or Sassoon's *Sherston's Progress*, for along with the sordidness and terror, he finds or thinks he finds portrayal of acts of heroism and comradeship. Not only is this true, but if a young person reads a convincing antiwar book, such as David Jones' *In Parenthesis*, he will dismiss it when the next war comes along by saying, "Oh, that was true about World War One or World War Two. But *this* is a different war. World War One was an imperialist war. This is an ideologic war." Or for the next war they will have another term. Perhaps "vindicated" or "intuitive" or "magnanimous." That is one of the dangers of language: it can always think of reasons. To the young people each war is "their war" and in a sense they're right . . . it is their war in the sense that they seize it. Men by their nature are inflammable. God knows *The Iliad* and *The Trojan Women* are adequately antiwar. If people had been going to change, they would have started a long time ago.

Griffin: To go back to the matter of the personal relation negating the political. . . . For those who are "immersed in the destructive element," that is, soldiers themselves, the personal always outweighs the political. For civilians, however, the opposite is true.

Auden: Quite. Whenever I talk about this, I think of my friend, Ross More, Second Army, Canadian Third Division. He was in the fighting at Caen and Bayeux. He couldn't fire a gun but he was sent out in the push that was made to capture Bayeux. He remembered taking a rug with him, because he didn't want to dirty his uniform, and he took a book. So sure enough he was wounded. He put down his rug and read until the bearers came and got him.

Griffin: One sees quite clearly this dichotomy between the personal and the political relation in *Macbeth*.

Auden: Yes, it is made clear at the very beginning of the play. The execution of the treacherous thane of Cawdor is different from the killing of Duncan. Duncan says:

Is execution done on Cawdor? Are not
Those in commission yet return'd?

Malcolm answers that Cawdor confessed and repented and
has been killed. Then Duncan:

There's no art
To find the mind's construction in the face.

This remark shows there is no personal relation involved
here. It is a political type of death, and Cawdor himself has
wanted to give restitution. In contrast to this, Shakespeare
gives us the killing in war of young Siward. But in regard to
the death of Banquo Shakespeare carefully makes clear the
personal relations on the part of Macbeth and the two murderers, who are not merely instruments but are animated by
enmity and spite.

Griffin: Toward the end of the play one is aware of a
great need on Macbeth's part to establish some relation to
others if only through violence.

Auden: Yes, he has been guilty of murder; in the case of
Lady Macduff it is almost a gratuitous killing. In murder, the
murderer is unrelated to the injured party and therefore there
can be no restitution or forgiveness. Why are murderers often
said to see ghosts? It is because in a sense the murderer desires
not to be left alone with the consciousness of crime; it is an
attempt to have relation with the other. In any other injury,
you can always think of the injured being in the world, and, if
you change your mind, you can ask for forgiveness.

Griffin: I think this passage is one of the keys of the play:

But let the frame of things disjoint, both the worlds suffer,
Ere we will eat our meal in fear, and sleep
In the affliction of these terrible dreams
That shake us nightly, better be with the dead,
Whom we, to gain our peace, have sent to peace,
Than on the torture of the mind to lie
In restless ecstasy.

Auden: Macbeth and his wife tried to be murderers without malice and therefore they become isolated from society because of crime. It is a case of treachery within the group. Macbeth cannot sleep. Neither can he forget because there is no one else to remember. Unable to enter the childish world of wish and dream (because the wish has become a fact) he must remain in the present. The past is related only to him and to no other. . . . "Better be with the dead. . . ."

Griffin: The latter part of the play is full of portentous and weary atmosphere. . . .

Auden: Yes, Macbeth begins to be sick of the sun. He thinks of the situations when the persons he killed were not to him *persons*. He desires that now. Why doesn't he commit suicide? In the last analysis he wants justice; he wants relation to his fellow men from whom he is cut off. If he commits suicide he denies relation. If he is killed, then in that act relation is restored.

Griffin: Lady Macbeth is believed to have committed suicide.

Auden: Because she has incited the trouble. She is more guilty in intention than Macbeth. Being more lonely than her husband, she refuses a relation. Since she has no direct relation with the victim, no way exists by which she can be reconciled. The reason Macbeth in the third act calls up Banquo's ghost is precisely that it is not Banquo, that it is not conscious, that no relation is possible.

Auden spoke of books about World War I, mentioning In Parenthesis *as one of the best and commenting on* Sherston's Progress:

Auden: Sassoon's book is interesting because he gives an idea of the officer-ordinary soldier relation in the British army. One difference exists between the British and the American army. The British officer usually has a better education; he feels more responsibility for his men, whereas the American officer is ordinarily less intelligent than the enlisted man. He is afraid this will be shown up and tries to hide it

18

by terrific arrogance. American officers incessantly quibble about rank and promotion. In the British army, one finds plenty of bitching about the food, quarters, etc. but less about rank.

Griffin: I wonder about this superior sense of responsibility. Do you think an analogous responsibility exists on the part of the English upper classes in regard to the lower strata?

Auden: To a certain extent. The attitude of a squire to those who work his land is parallel. England has a tradition of noblesse oblige.

Griffin: It is mostly the noblesse who believe in that tradition.

Auden: A good British army officer does feel a definite sense of obligation toward his men. You see it in the Sassoon book.

Griffin: Yes, but I think Sassoon was an exception. His relation with his servant, a private, was very close and without friction. But I can imagine that such a relation might many times have been anything but that.

Auden: As an officer Sassoon regarded his company as a family and himself as the head of it.

Griffin: There is a tendency to say "the officer and the men"; the men are conceived as a homogeneous unit, as a lump, not as a group of individuals with their rights.

Auden: In this connection the definition of "gentlemen" is interesting. According to English law a gentleman is a "respectable man who engages in no occupation or profession for gain." In time of war an English gentleman automatically becomes an officer. By knowing the right people and coming from the correct stratum of society things are made quite easy for such a person. He has the angels on his side to begin with: you see that with Sassoon. In his case he did not misuse his advantages.

Griffin: In a sense I think the British army is more provincial than the American.

19

Auden: Why?

Griffin: I noticed that in Japan the GI became a sightseer. But Tommy Atkins is never a sightseer.

Auden: Does this mean he is more provincial?

Griffin: Wherever he goes the Britisher projects his world. A clearing in the jungle allows him to set up a bridge table. He brings England with him. Despite his narrowness, I think the American is more resilient and open to outside influences. He is sympathetically curious about other people. Set down in some outpost the Tommy spends his leisure imagining what's going on back in Sussex. Given the chance to choose between a trip to Kashmir, say, and a get-together with chaps from his part of Sussex, the Tommy will choose the latter.

Auden: This business of being detached depends largely on psychic factors. I am, I suppose, something of a *déraciné* and with me it is mostly a matter of temperament. How strongly one identifies oneself with the land depends, too, on how soon one falls into a family pattern. . . .

Griffin: You mentioned "Strange Meeting." Do you think any poet has been produced by the last war comparable to Owen?

Auden: No. It is ironical that his stuff written about one war served as the only adequate commentary on the next, even though the method of fighting was outmoded in the interim. Due to the change in type of warfare, almost no good poetry has come out of this war. I doubt if the sort of mind required for a combat pilot or a bombardier is capable of producing good poetry.

Griffin: It is very difficult to write about the actual experience of fighting.

Auden: Yes. I think the best account of a battle was given by Captain Strahan. He saw action at Cherbourg and Bastogne. After being wounded, he was sent back to England. When a reporter asked him what the Battle of Bastogne was like he said, "Oh, my dear fellow, *the noise . . . and the people!*"

Griffin: What amazes me in so many of your poems, even your very early poems, is the way you foretold, or foreshadowed, so many later developments. You saw the war coming and you spoke about it clearly.

Auden: Oh, yes, prophecies, but one doesn't mean them really. It's as if one said, "It will rain tomorrow." Perhaps as it happens, it does, but one only said it because it rhymed with sorrow.

Griffin: In connection with *The Ascent of F.6*, I would like to ask you a question about the protagonist. Was that figure based on Colonel Lawrence?

Auden: Yes. The ascent of the mountain is a symbol of the *geste*; it can also be a symbol of the act of aggression.

Griffin: Then you look on Lawrence definitely as a jingoist?

Auden: Oh no, he was surely in sympathy with the Arabs.

Griffin: Yes, but only up to a point. He concurred with England's imperialist policies. Also, he regarded war as a game, a sport—

Auden: There is a difference between regarding war as a sport and being jingoistic. With the business of unconditional surrender, modern warfare cannot be regarded as a game. Not since the eighteenth century has it really been possible to compare war to a game. During wars like the last two, officers and RA men wanted the fighting to be over so they could get back to "real soldiering." They resented the intrusion of civilians into the forces, despite the fact that they usually made superior soldiers. Only to fighter pilots war might appear as a game because there one has the business of individual scoring.

Griffin: You believe, don't you, that there were real ideologic factions involved in the last war?

Auden: Yes, in regard to Germany. In regard to Japan, however, it was imperialistic. But most people really believed that Germany was wrong and should be stopped. . . .

All Hitler's actions cannot be explained logically. That is why Chamberlain failed at Munich. Since he was a typical businessman, he judged Hitler from a practical point of view. Because Hitler had most of Europe at his feet, Chamberlain could not see how he could want more. There is a perversity in people that makes it unwise to try to explain all their actions in terms of economic advantage. How artificial a basis of society money is can be seen in the dilemma of the Spanish colonists who, when they came to this country, could not get the Indians to do enough work for them. They would work to get just enough for subsistence. Beyond that they would not work because it interfered with their leisure. . . .

. . . Wars are fought over geographic frontiers; there is no particular reason why they should be. It is a convention that makes of an arbitrary line a moral thing. It says, for instance, that if you cross from one zone to another you are punishable. The idea of national sovereignty confirms this fictional belief in strict boundaries. The concept of national sovereignty can be indirectly attacked by recommending the abolition of passport control and immigration laws. This would be a good thing. If passports were junked and a certain country declared war, one could just leave the country. Consequently governments would have to make it desirable for people to live within their jurisdiction.

Griffin: But wouldn't there be overconcentrations, then, in attractive areas?

Auden: Things would even themselves out. One can trust the great inertia of the human race.

Griffin: It might create a vast floating population.

Auden: That would be all right, too. Let people move around. Of course, most men are much too lazy to shop around for a country to live in. All this fuss over world government. It seems so simple to me. You just have to throw all passports in the sea, and tax incomes at the source.

Griffin: I'd like to go back to a remark you made earlier.

You said that you thought the British officer quibbled less about rank than the American officer. How would you compare the German and the American officer?

Auden: The German exercised more initiative and original thinking than his British or American counterpart. The cream of the American army were the sergeants. The officers I met talked exactly like big wheels at an NAM meeting. The difference between the English and the Germans is shown in that story about the rowing meet. In preparation the Germans performed feats of training and spent considerable time, but the English arrived on the scene half drunk and in confusion. The event commenced and the Germans at first outdistanced their opponents but toward the end of the contest while the English were going under a bridge, someone spat on them. At this time they became so mad that they rowed terrifically and won the race.

Griffin: The English think it is bad form to be too serious.

Auden: My brother is a mountain climber; he is a very good one and has been on many expeditions. But he used to complain about the attitude of the Germans. All they think about is getting to the top.

Griffin: Many Americans waxed indignant over the race-superiority myths of the Germans, yet were we to be honest, we would have to admit the existence here of a master and a slave race.

Auden: There is more real racism in this country than there was in Germany at the height of Goebbels' power. The feeling against the Jew is not primarily economic. The Jews think Christians are too frivolous; the Christians think Jews are too serious—but serious about the wrong things. Christians feel about Jews the way Englishmen do about the Scotch. The Scotch work too hard; they're clannish, industrious, too religious and they think they're the apple of God's eye. They seldom have a sense of humor.

Griffin: Or you might use as a parallel the way the English feel about the Irish?

Auden: No, that is different. We feel that the Irish are right—but they talk too much about it. Many Jews go to Eton; nothing is thought of that. We had a Jewish prime minister; that could not happen here. In an English school, scholars would be divided as to whether their parents were in trade or in the professions. The Jewish persons in England, and there are many, have been well assimilated. The anti-Negro feeling in America, however, is mainly economic. When you talk to one of the more rabid Southerners you find that what he wants to do is to keep the Negro in his place. But when you talk to an anti-Semite you find he wants the Jew not to *be*. It is the difference between exploitation and annihilation. . . .

Griffin: Do you think one's early education should place much emphasis on forms and social manners?

Auden: In a capitalist democracy too little attention is paid to manners. People are born serious, selfish and honest. Through suffering, they must learn to become frivolous and insincere. In order that we may not take ourselves as seriously as a baby does, we have to learn to be serious about other people. First of all, we are trained not to claim the attention of others; when we do, we have to deserve it. In social intercourse when we speak we have a duty to be funny and we mustn't talk too long. Lack of convention leaves any society at the mercy of its most selfish member. In the absence of a code of manners, it is extremely difficult to know what relations are developing between you and the people you meet. How problematical it is at a cocktail party where people you have never met before behave as if they knew you very well! If a convention of social action exists, however, slight departures from it tell you how you are changing in relation with someone else. We have to remember that we cannot trust our own feelings and so a code of behavior tides us over. We have to bear in mind that we are a great deal less interested in others than we like to admit. In manners we pretend to be concerned about people we never wish to see again.

Griffin: The dramatic poet, I think, is guilty of a certain type of dishonesty.

Auden: He is honest with himself and deceives others. . . . But God knows one can't have honesty in human relationships! The most dishonest people are those who are unaware they are acting. To be honest with oneself means to know oneself as an actor, not to take oneself too seriously. You can, therefore, be honest with yourself and deceive others. Kierkegaard, for instance. You can be honest with others and deceive yourself. Don Quixote takes himself too seriously—particularly at first. That is why he needs Sancho Panza—the reality-principle. Terrible things happen to Don Quixote because he refuses to know he is acting; but at last he learns to forgive. He tries to do good, to help people and just gets in their way. There is a third type of dishonesty— one can be dishonest altogether. Most persons in modern society are honest—that is, frank—with others and deceive themselves. But a convention of complete frankness amounts to nothing really but a form of dishonesty.

Griffin: Whom would you cite as an example of the third type of complete dishonesty?

Auden: Rousseau. With his theories of the Golden Age and the General Will he was, I think, responsible for totalitarianism in its modern form. His ideas of the deification of the State and Civil Religion became the weapons of the dictators. According to Rousseau, the noble savage is born good and free, becomes corrupted by institutions—

Griffin: And you believe that some of the blame should be placed on man himself?

Auden: Absolutely. Since it is he who makes the institutions. I think that the first step toward the realization of a universal good society is a belief in the fall of man.

Griffin: Would you explain that?

Auden: The Christian story of the Fall teaches that no

man is really much better than any other. Which does not, however, hinder you from choosing between two things in particular cases, say, between two men up for office, and deciding A is better suited than B, but it does act as a safeguard against idolizing or entrenching any particular man.

Griffin: Do you believe that power inevitably corrupts?

Auden: Politics brings out different gifts in a man than other fields do. A surgeon, for instance, has power over other lives yet is not corrupted by it. A leader may start out with humanitarian feelings, yet when he gets to the top he is corrupted by his position. All totalitarian societies start out as utopias . . .

I believe pretty much in the platonic idea of inborn traits. Not that, of course, I have faith in a static sort of society. But there is an extreme slipperiness about a capitalist democracy that is not good. Here there are thousands of persons desiring to be that for which they have no talent, longing to be movie stars, for instance. They'd be happier staying home but they do not realize this. A society should have just enough flexibility for each man to move around and find his right spot. Most people in America do not know what they have a talent for: they have become A Wish. Also, they are not willing really to work and to concentrate. Americans, you know, are not efficient. If you have ever been to a faculty meeting you know that. They have an amount of business to do that could be done in an hour and they waste the whole afternoon doing it, because if they finish it earlier, what are they going to do with the time? The English would accomplish just as much in half the time.

Griffin: Another illustration of your point, I think, is the American love of gadgets. Americans use gadgets to save time which is spent in the operation of other time-saving gadgets. The device comes to be a time-filler in itself. It creates leisure but Americans are embarrassed by leisure.

Auden: Or else they think it wicked.

Griffin: We have strayed from our starting point. . . .

Auden: Yes, to go back to the use of power. . . . I think it might be a good idea if political jobs were granted by lot or by universal regulation like jury duty. Everyone should be made to serve at some time. It would be a nuisance but it would be good.

Griffin: What would you say about the infliction of punishment by lot? Judge Lindsey claimed that every year a lottery should be held to decide who should go to prison and who should not. He said that the result would be as impartial as our present justice and would also give each an opportunity to be punished and reformed as a miserable sinner. God would keep an eye on the matter to see that those who had not drawn a bad lot would get what they deserved.

Auden: We cannot rely on God to that extent. He nods. As for its being as impartial as our present justice, that's probably true. It is true that everyone has done wrong things and it does seem unfair to make individuals expiators for society. But one must remember that a certain amount of punishment acts as a deterrent. Anyway that is only an external attack on what is essentially an inward problem. It places—as did Rousseau—too large a blame on the institution. The Christian theologians are more nearly right when they blame man himself for his pride and his refusal to accept suffering. Man is perverse to the extent that he is capable of enjoying the toothache; he may take pleasure in not loving his neighbor.

Griffin: Would you agree that one of the errors of psychoanalysis is that it places too great an emphasis on knowledge as a corrective of behavior?

Auden: Yes. Men are not deterred from doing a particular act, though they know it is harmful to society or to themselves. In *Notes from Underground* Dostoyevsky gives the classic illustration of this. Surely, the psychiatrist proves to me that my act is unsocial; still I choose it to show my autonomy. Sociologists and psychiatrists both treat man as if he were a logical entity.

Griffin: Do you think they classify people too neatly?

Auden: For the most part they let you classify yourself. Why are people neurotic? Because they refuse to accept suffering. Psychiatrists err in several directions: too often they assume they can change people. . . . Freud said he wasn't interested in changing people. In your dealings with psychiatrists, you may find yourself in a false situation. You go to one of them attracted by his claim to free you, to unchain you from your fears and obsessions, but after talking to him for a while you discover that he himself is not free: he is ruled by an interest in money.

Griffin: Do you believe that psychiatry should be used in the treatment of criminals?

Auden: Very little. If a murderer knows that all that will happen to him is a few sessions with a psychiatrist, why he'll be murdering people right and left.

How would the psychiatrist attack the problem? If he says to the thief: Oh you poor boy, your mother did not love you or she loved you too much and that is why you steal, he's going to go right on stealing.

Griffin: True, but there are certain crimes—infanticide, parricide, etc.—which can be clarified by psychiatric research.

Auden: A great deal depends, too, on the periphery in which an offense is performed. If I see an expensive book in a store, I may steal it. I may see the same book in a friend's house and not be tempted for two reasons: (1) I know he'll miss it and suspect me, (2) I can see very clearly the hurt it will give him.

Griffin: In the South Sea islands they say it is possible to maintain a peaceable life with the minimum of taboos.

Auden: Manifestly because of the restriction of the periphery. To give a different example: one needs more taboos in a city than in a family. In a family the withdrawal of affection may form sufficient punishment. But in a city no. Say a thief is caught. One cannot punish his crime by the withdrawal of affection, that in fact may have been its cause.

Griffin: I get the impression that you think psychiatrists are too dictatorial in their methods?
Auden: Some of them are power-maniacs. About half of them are quacks. They think they have all the answers. I would much rather have the police in charge than psychiatrists. The police can always be bribed. The Chinese realize that. The poor people there buy the policeman's favor by flattering him, pulling him in the house, giving him a cup of tea, etc.... They believe it is their duty to corrupt the policeman by sending him gifts and doing services for him. They know that no policeman in the world can resist such attention. Even in a democracy the law enforcement is a dangerous profession; in dealing with crooks you become like them.
Griffin: Do you believe that the universal state should be preponderantly *Polizei* or *laissez faire?*
Auden: It must not be *Polizei.* The larger the government, the more scattered the people, then the less can force be relied on. Fouché was responsible for the origin of the police state. In order to see how amazingly it operated one has to go back to the First Empire and read about those times. It makes fascinating reading. Fouché started out as a Catholic, reacted violently and became an atheist. His life was a net of intrigue and he died immensely rich. He was opportunistic but never the tool of others. The direct descendant of his secret police exists in all totalitarian countries.... At first Napoleon and Fouché worked hand in glove. Not really surprising. Essentially Napoleon was an opportunist, a Machiavellian. He wanted to astonish his mother. He started out trying to make France prosperous but when he got power, he thought only of making Paris into Rome. He was a sentimentalist about himself and a cynic about everything else. His attitude toward missionaries, for instance, is amusing. He had extremely imperialistic ideas and thought he could use missionaries in Africa and Asia to expand his dominion. Using their apparent

sanctity as a decoy, he wanted to employ them as agents.

Griffin: You say Napoleon "wanted to astonish his mother." In your *New Year Letter*, I remember you have a passage on matriarchal influence:

Adits were entrances which led
Down to the Outlawed, to the Others,
The Terrible, the Merciful, the Mothers. . . .

And I am a little perplexed by the meaning of the mother-image which reveals itself on the mountain in *The Ascent of F.6*. . . .Would you explain more fully what you meant by that image?

Auden: It seems to me that in man's search for God he erects before him a number of images. I believe that the mother-image is one of the last to be outgrown. . . . In this play the protagonist dies after the appearance of the mother on the mountaintop.

Griffin: With the insight of Freud, Shakespeare shows us that Coriolanus is motivated—partly at least—by a desire to "astonish his mother." He makes quite clear the blood-thirsty, terrible, severe attitude of the mother in speeches like

Volumnia: To a cruel war I sent him, from whence he return'd, his brows bound with oak. I tell thee, daughter, I sprang not more in joy at first hearing he was a manchild than now in first seeing he had proved himself a man.

Virgilia: But had he died in the business, madam, how then?

Volumnia: Then his good report should have been my son; I therein would have found issue.

Auden: Don't you think that in a curious way this sacrificial willingness on the part of parents has been out-moded? Fortunately or unfortunately, the new type of warfare disallows such clear-cut distinctions. In atomic war there can be no question of mothers sitting in a room somewhere, sewing and visualizing (like Volumnia) the bestial and distant actions of her son. Our weapons have made it impossible for the few to send others into the wilderness to atone for them. There is no desert to lead men into now except everywhere.

Auden: True. Death has become that which it has never been: what may happen *to me* as a person. But one must admit the role of the parent is a difficult one, particularly in these days of technological "preventive" war. If I had children, I would want them to be either physicists or ballet dancers. Then they'd always have a job.

three

Griffin (*gesturing toward a newspaper*):   Did you read the Victor Caine story?

Auden: Oh yes. Messy. I must confess *crimes passionels* bore me. It is the repetition, the lack of imagination that's so tiresome. There are so many Victor Caines, and of course they're unbalanced in a way that might have been cleared up. The intensity of emotion is what creates legends but the intensity alone cannot create the legend. Look at how a legend gets started. Here you have a young man who, because of his intense feeling, killed his wife and himself and it's conceivable, if a Dante or Malory came along, he might be made into a legend. One can't talk, in this connection, of right and wrong. If the love is very intense, it somehow resolves itself in death.

Griffin: Do you feel that a kind of erotic love has an affinity with death? Let us say this love has existed and has grown less intense, do you think that the endurance of life then only cheapens and tarnishes the love?

Auden: Yes, in a way. A courage is required to pursue love to its logical violence, to make a type of emotion inevitable. But the raw material is boring. Very unpleasant. Behind them they leave an untidy mess for other people. This was true of Paolo and Francesca, of Antony and Cleopatra. They left a lot of blood stains and loose ends and it was a nasty job for other people to straighten things up. The straightening-up, I believe, has to go on and I sympathize with those who have to do it. Take, for instance, the case of Paolo and Francesca. If it had not been for a poet, Paolo would have been forgotten like Victor Caine. There

32

was this contemporary Dante, who heard of the incident and saw how it might fit into a long poem he was considering. About people like Paolo and Francesca, and Antony and Cleopatra, there's a great deal, really, of the police-court or psychiatric clinic case.

Griffin: Why are *crimes passionels* committed? Out of, would you say, "love" or "sexual passion"?

Auden: No. Rather because an individual confuses a human being with a thing. He regards a living spirit as only an obstruction, an object.

Griffin: According to you, then, the poets have invented the idea of romantic love?

Auden: That's putting it too simply. Given a historical situation, it can be looked at in three ways: from the point of view of the realist, romanticist, or ironist. You mentioned the case of Paolo and Francesca. What does the realist see in the whole affair?—here is a particularly callous marriage of convenience. Francesca's father, in order to cement a political alliance, arranges to marry off his daughter to an influential lord, Gianciotto Malatesta, but the latter being deformed, his brother, a good-looking lad called Paolo, is sent instead to clinch the details of the deal. What happens? By means of deliberate misrepresentation Francesca is led to believe that Paolo himself is the suitor and does not discover the deception until her wedding night. All the arrangements of Gianciotto have meanwhile become disturbed by something which cannot be arranged: the existence of love. Although Francesca marries Gianciotto, Paolo, who himself is married and has been for four years, seems to be living now and then under the same roof with his brother and what is inevitable begins to happen: he starts sleeping with his brother's wife, but this incestuous relation is eventually betrayed through the agency of a servant. Gianciotto on surprising them in bed kills them, pinning them together with one sword-thrust. At this time, Francesca had a daughter nine years old. Paolo was thirty-six. After this violent deed, Gianciotto with dispatch returned to his affairs. He was involved in military campaigns and built several great fortresses. Not long afterward he married a widow from whom he had five children. These are the facts, not the facts of love, but they're the facts. It's history. The facts of love are very impressive and are different.

Griffin: Capetanakis said somewhere: "In love the dry facts do not tell much; one must know what the facts meant to the lovers, how the lovers lived the facts—"

Auden: That's true. You know, I'm not trying to debunk something. The facts of love are not articulate facts; they are values. They are an accident of touch, perhaps, or a tone of voice or a glance. Let me be clear that I'm not talking about what historical novelists or poetasters invent about a certain relation but rather about something very precise; "the facts of love" are immediate and have a temporal existence. You'll not find them written down in the family chronicles and old records but they were realities, as strong and actual as Gianciotto's fortresses. It all lies in the pathos of that verb "were." Endowed with a gift to see the temporal situation under the aspect of eternity, the great poet comes along and he creates something like the fifth canto of *The Inferno* which, though nearer to the facts of love, is different. Consider now the second point of view, the romanticist's. In this connection, the romanticist is a personification of the popular imagination. The facts take on a temporal form in an old record or an oral tradition and if they happen to have great universal appeal, the popular imagination will seize upon them. Because of its vulgar nature the popular imagination sees little more than it wants to see; it is wishful and tends to project. But it has great strength—

Griffin: And hence the legend, the historical novel, the illustrious example.

Auden: Now let's glance at the third point of view, that of the ironist. The limitations of a situation loom larger to him than the situation itself. Of course he has more sophistication and insight than the romanticist but he tends to concentrate on a situation at the point where things start to go wrong. He has a good eye for contradiction. Given a set of circumstances, he would not want to poetize them but, on the other hand, he does not want to understand them for that might involve an effort of feeling and a glance into the darker side of life. The ironist desires to put the terrible situation in its place.

Griffin: He has, then, a hatred of extremity? In the story of Paolo and Francesca, he'd be interested in the fact that Paolo at his death had been married fourteen years and had two children. He would make much of the fact that Paolo and Francesca carried on their affair ten years before they were discovered. The ironist would be greatly interested in what might be called the continuance-principle; he'd fasten his attention on contingency. The ironist is not the flippant person who is usually hopeless but he is the person who turns away from the dark side of life. The daily round to him is pitiful and full of change; he never hears the music underneath the earth.

Auden: In his outlook the great poet fuses all three attitudes and makes of them a unique attitude of his own which posterity will then call "Shakespearean" or "Dantesque." The tragic poet can employ irony but the ironist is never the tragic poet. Consider the later plays of Shakespeare. In them nothing is simplified. You see man portrayed in the middle register, not altogether good or altogether bad. He shows us how, when the order of the world is fairly good, bad individuals come to disturb the surface and set up change, and, on the other hand, when the order is bad, it's continually being softened by the virtue of particular men.

Griffin: *Antony and Cleopatra* is a good example of that—

Auden: This is one of the most complex plays Shakespeare wrote. Even in his high vein, this play verges now and then on the absurd—

Griffin: It's an intricate study in character.

Auden: And Antony steals the show.—We're told that he's noble. His spirit (the Soothsayer declares) is "courageous, high, unmatchable." Cleopatra sings his praises, but all this remains a verbal tribute—

Griffin: Part of the fascination of the play lies in the disparity between the tissue of praise and the actuality of the man.

Auden: And this disparity, like a crack in the surface of this whole world, soon becomes apparent—

Griffin: He does not seem highly ambitious in terms of self, though he may be a little jealous of Ventidius. As a man he has great power over other men.

Auden: Yes, the gladiators, you recall, bravely try to join his forces, working their way through Galatia and Syria in an effort to reach him at Alexandria. And that after Actium, too. Antony has, in this play, a wonderfully magnetic quality which, above all, a leader needs. Antony is an unreflective, simple person. An old campaigner. Something of a visceral type.

Griffin: If one used the category of the humors, one would place him as of the phlegmatic disposition. He has none of the misanthropy of Hamlet or Timon. His emotions—of anger, passion, scorn—lie close to the surface. He's strongly sexed, and with his large faults he towers over everyone in the play, over the rationalizing Pompey, the spiteful Octavius who is cruel and cautious—

Auden: Over Cleopatra?

Griffin: Even over Cleopatra. At the end his death has a quality of will and grandeur which hers lacks. None of the fatal qualities in his nature are shirked by Shakespeare—we see he's attracted by liquor and good food. He loves to get plastered and sleep it off. After the naval defeat, when Antony confronts the queen, he says:

We sent our schoolmaster;
Is 'a come back? Love, I am full of lead.
Some wine, within there, and our viands!

36

In these lines you see the distraction of his mind. He's finished and he knows it—

Auden: Yes, he knows he's finished. Antony and Cleopatra are hopeless people who are beginning to lose their grip. The historical predicament counters the inner problem.

Griffin: Do you think Shakespeare is particularly interested in showing how public and private history interact?

Auden: Yes. Antony's caught in this struggle for the domination of the civilized world, a struggle that, with the triumph of Octavius, was to result in the Egypto-Roman Empire. Antony and Cleopatra *are caught* in a way not true of Octavius or Julius Caesar. Essentially they are ordinary human beings who're interested in worldly things more than in conquest. If their fate is more spectacular than usual, it is because they have been very successful for a while.

Griffin: In Alexandria, Antony and Cleopatra tried to form a society of two, an Amimetobion, an "Inimitable Life." This society, of course, could not last, being doomed by its exclusiveness, and the "news from Rome" is the symbol of the outward threat. But since this society was, in its way, a Golden Age it lead finally to a we-are-sunk feeling.

Auden: So much of *Antony and Cleopatra* concerns the reaction of the individual to what the existentialists call "frontier-" or "limit-situations." The story takes place on the frontier of the civilized world and, thematically, it is concerned with the psychic frontiers, with suffering, finiteness, conflict, guilt, sex and death. As you know, the existentialists believe that the frontier-situation brings the individual up against an awareness of his dependent nature. It jolts him to a recognition of his aloneness and vulnerability, like a missing step in a stair. In this play the protagonists react to their predicament in such a manner that, at the end, they achieve self-transcendence.

Griffin: To a remarkable extent, certain scenes in *Antony and Cleopatra* reek with the atmosphere of death, sleep, and drunkenness.

Auden: You might describe this play as the struggle to realize a "personal death." Neither Mark Antony nor his queen are attracted to suffering which, like solitude, seems to them meaningless if not ridiculous.

Griffin: But Antony is no libertine. He does not act only according to his impulses and physical desires. Even Octavius admits:

> Thou didst drink
> The stale of horses and the gilded puddle
> Which beasts would cough at.

In his nature, there is no mean; he swings from hunger to surfeit; from vicissitude to extreme luxury. He wants to push his life as far as it will go. After Actium, the historical Antony went into retirement and lived in the house of the port official, the Timoneum; here he remained alone, fishing a little, gazing out at the harbor. Surprisingly, he seems not to have minded living alone, not seeing Cleopatra, aware of the lights of her palace blazing across the water, catching sometimes the sounds of revelry and music from that direction . . . . And toward the end of the play Antony does suffer. Shakespeare makes that apparent in such a speech as:

> But when we in our viciousness grow hard—
> O misery on 't!—the wise gods seel our eyes,
> In our own filth drop our clear judgments

A case could be made out for *Antony and Cleopatra* as a pageant-play about the great world, revolving around the ideas of sex and death.

Auden: Yes, sex is in back of it all.

Griffin: Sex is in back of *Romeo and Juliet*, too.

Auden: Yes, but look at the difference. There's a difference in matter and in form. We find in *Romeo and Juliet* a youthful love story. The protagonists wish to escape from the family to a society of two, world of the remote cottage.

This play concerns the discovery that sexual love exists by which they realize their selves. It's a boy meets girl plot, the obstruction: a row without political significance. It happens to have been an old family feud but it could've been anything, as people have a dispute over who borrowed the lawn mower. On the other hand, Antony and Cleopatra (who, incidentally, are scarcely young) cannot be imagined as retiring to a cottage: their affair must be lived in the blaze of attention.

In *Romeo and Juliet* you find the pure Petrarchan love-rhetoric out of the book. Being inexperienced the progatonists must use this; they are at the stage of trying to imagine what they feel. Since love to them is new, they must go to the books to describe it, but love to Antony and Cleopatra is an old game.

> Antony: I found you as a morsel cold upon
> Dead Caesar's trencher; nay, you were a fragment
> On Gneius Pompey's; besides what hotter hours,
> Unregister'd in vulgar fame, you have
> Luxuriously pick'd out.

In order to establish feeling, Antony and Cleopatra try to test the love-convention. In Cleopatra's case particularly, it's important for her to prove she can feel. "Think on me, that am with Phoebus' amorous pinches black." Largely, sensuality has destroyed her feeling but it's necessary for her to inspire feelings in others: that's why she has to behave so badly. When Antony rebels against loss of feeling, he escapes into drinking. We find in this play a poetic diction conscious of exaggeration. The characters employ the word to foreshadow feeling about which they're in doubt and to make themselves important. When they quarrel, they experience hate inspired by fear. What they are secretly saying is not like Romeo and Juliet: *How grand to feel like this!* but: *I want to live forever.* The poetic expression is a technique for keeping up the excitement. Antony and Cleopatra remain more selfish with clearer knowledge of that than Romeo and Juliet.

Griffin: Isn't it true that since, as you say, sensuality has numbed Cleopatra's capacity for feeling, she is now interested in prestige and success? To achieve her ends she must make a pretense of love with Antony, but her free employment of the word "love" usually covers strivings of power. She is aggressive—

Auden: Aggressive but, at times, curiously unable to cope. She says to Enobarbus: "What shall we do?"

Griffin: She desires to exploit Antony. She could not have the same relation with a handsome centurion as she does with the Roman conqueror. Cleopatra is Egypt; Antony, landlord of this world.

Auden: But Antony is landlord of the world only for a while, and their relationship continues after that.

Griffin: La Rochefoucauld has a maxim where he makes a distinction between the type of lover who's crazy with love and the lover who's more of a sot. There is something of the sot in Antony.

Auden: However, he's not a Lucio. Shakespeare seems to have regarded sexual indulgence as an evil excess of something good in itself. In Antony there is great indulgence but not without its consciousness and a sense of transgression. Antony and his queen want to escape from old age and death, from the future, that is, but not from the world, not from people—which is the reason there must be attendants, musicians, courtiers everywhere, the coming and going of messengers. When the sexual experience becomes less a physical need than a way of forgetting time and death, it becomes destructive and it doesn't work.

Griffin: Sexuality is woven like a thread through the whole play. As early as the second scene there's the speech:

Soothsayer: You shall be more beloving than belov'd.
Chairman: I had rather heat my liver with drinking.

Auden: Drinking, of course, can be a bid for affection, for absolute tolerance. It's certainly connected with getting stuck or sold out, emotionally.

Griffin: And the talk of the maids about "the inch of fortune" seems in character.

Auden: They're trying to make the future, accidental as it seems to them, more concrete in sexual terms. People like Charmian and Iras make a great deal of luck which represents for them what military fortune does for Scarus and Ventidius.

Griffin: To Cleopatra these two worlds may be equated. What difference whether she plays politics with Octavius or at billiards with the eunuch? She is bored. Boredom becomes the constant negative of her affair with Antony—

Auden: —as it is of his affair with her.

Griffin: Ennui is the refusal to learn from the past. Because she cannot act, Cleopatra is more bored than Antony:

Cleopatra: As well a woman with an eunuch played
As with a woman. Come, you'll play with me, sir?
Mardian: As well as I can, madam.

Auden: Cleopatra "trades in love." Her affairs with Caesar and later with Antony are expedient.

Griffin: Historically, she's supposed to have [tried to captivate] Octavius.

Auden: Yes; she kills herself not because Antony, whom she did love, is dead but because Dolabella, who's attracted to her—even in her state of past youth, tells her Caesar will humiliate her and kill her son. Antony does not commit suicide because Cleopatra is represented as dead; he's already decided to do so. Enobarbus has gone against him in a way that parallels Cleopatra's treachery. Neither Antony nor his queen knows how to grow old. At the end Cleopatra is thirty-nine; Antony, fifty-four. He's turning gray and would be putting on weight; she has to make up very carefully indeed. Quite consciously they have adopted public masks.

41

In this situation public life has assumed the place of parents and taken away their freedom.

Griffin: Antony cuts rather the figure of a rebel boy. He wants the freedom to play that, as a child, he had. Because of loss of innocence, he cannot be a child or a private citizen again. When he challenges Octavius to single combat, it is not fatuous or absurd; it is one of the magnificent gestures of the play. Cleopatra sees in Antony the great hero who has become sated and can be overruled. She despises him for letting her dominate him. Octavius she can't get; anyway, he'd dominate her. She has the power to destroy a man who has something to lose.

Auden: As a youth Antony did not shine in scholastic things. Now in revenge he uses the schoolmaster as war-messenger. Obviously, Euphronius should be occupied with the teaching of Antony's children; instead he's dispatched as envoy to Octavius. For Antony is a person who lives in the immediate not in the real. The messenger tells Antony "The nature of bad news infects the teller" but Antony will have none of this: "Things that are past are done with me." The truly strong man, he believes, acts in the present. He refuses to see—to do so would bring him face to face with his conflict—that the past continues living in the present and constantly changing him. Antony's naive conception of time ruins him as a strategist against the more sophisticated Octavius, who can wait. Things are only changed, Antony believes, by seizure of the moment. He does not talk of his life with Fulvia, his background; he never speaks of his sons.

Griffin: I'm glad you mentioned the messenger. For the messengers in this play have important roles. They give an effect of urgency and tumult; and tie the Egypto-Roman world together. In this play space is the prize, not a particular corner of space but the space of civilization; the enemy being time, time in the sense of age and the fluctuating of the spirit. In *Antony and Cleopatra* Shakespeare has gotten past history *moralisé*. We don't find here neat rhetorical abstractions: son

42

slaying father; father slaying son. He employs now a quick impressionist manner with many changes of scene (a technique perhaps suggested by Plutarch), where everything is confined to what is necessary. Time is seen not as the teacher but the enemy to love, the loosener of ties, the bringer of wrinkles. More of a "gypsy" than Cleopatra, Antony lives "fast and loose"; he is concerned with "the minute of life stretched with pleasure." Shakespeare develops the opposition between love-time and war-time. On the other hand, Antony is defeated by another temporality. A brilliant improviser and a good general, he cannot plan a long-term strategy. However, he does feel a certain responsibility: "Let mischief work." The "child o' the time" has little patience. By his impersonal slowness and caution Octavius undoes the brilliant improviser.

Auden: In connection with the messengers note how they're treated. They are important as links, but also as whipping-boys.

Griffin: They have to take a lot of crap. So do reporters nowadays—

Auden: A real difference exists. The messenger, then, was he who brought the communication to the ruler not interested in communication. Above all, Antony does not want to hear what the couriers have to say. In those days the bringer of bad news, because of a confusion of fortune and the instrumentality of fortune, might be put to death.

Griffin: But in back of all this was a refusal of connection. If you kill the messenger, you make the messenger responsible rather than yourself. Being a sensual animal, Cleopatra would like to destroy the messenger who brings her the news of Antony's marriage. But she does not destroy him; instead she says, afterward,

> Pity me, Charmian,
> But do not speak to me.

She is interested in emotion; she has little interest in communication.

Auden: Later, Shakespeare makes her reflect:

These hands do lack nobility, that they strike
A meaner than myself; since I myself
Have given myself the cause.

This halfawareness of the situation is rare for her but this happens to be the fact and, in spite of her anger, Cleopatra has a woman's respect for facts.

Griffin: She is, we are told, "cunning past man's thought." She is unreliable but—rewarding. During a time of indecision, Antony says: "Would I had never seen her!" and Enobarbus answers: "O, sir, you had then left unseen a wonderful piece of work, which not to have been blest withal would have discredited your travel." The ironic note cannot be missed—

Auden: —but he's also saying: It was imprudent to know Cleopatra, but prudence is not everything.

PART II

Griffin: You mentioned, earlier, that Shakespeare seems to regard sex as a good—

Auden: It seems to him more than neutral, it is a good but it can become an evil—

Griffin: Through enslavement?

Auden: When known as a matter of course, sex continues the race, but when known in the way that Antony and Cleopatra have known it, it exists as a characteral force, dark and powerful.

Griffin: In contrasting this play with *Romeo and Juliet*, you said, a while back, that Antony and Cleopatra could never be imagined as retiring; they must live in the fullest possible publicity.

Auden: Yes, lovers like Romeo and Juliet would like to find the private landscape, the enchanted cottage, the Atlantic City hotel. Of course, they can't; it is the project of something interior. But Antony and Cleopatra need the maximum assistance from clothes, liquor and other externals; they require expensive food, solicitous servants. We know it's the last affair for both of them.

Griffin: Romeo and Juliet deeply trust each other and, if one asks: Had they married and gone on, would they have been happy? No one can answer. But Antony and Cleopatra do not trust each other a yard. Little doubt exists for them what will happen. Cleopatra is less a fatalist than an opportunist. Antony feels that the future will condemn him—

Auden: Only toward the end of the play. In the first scene, you recall, the old veteran [Philo says of Antony]:

Take but good note, and you shall see in him
The triple pillar of the world transform'd
Into a strumpet's fool. Behold and see.
    Cleopatra: If it be love indeed, tell me how much.
    Antony: There's beggary in the love that can be reckon'd.

This rhetoric has not much value but what lies in back of the talk is, of course, sex; and the sex experience, when known in the way that Antony and Cleopatra have known it, faces the individual with a choice. Consciously or unconsciously it forces him to choose between love, the continuance of sex with tenderness and other emotions added, or death, self-destruction, the suicide pact or the living death of repetition. You see how in the lines quoted Cleopatra "words" her lover but then, on the other hand, the old veteran does not have all the right on his side. Antony is a great deal more than "a strumpet's fool." Knowing the complexity of the soul, Shakespeare never says: This person is this. That person is that.

Griffin: But one thing we're sure of: Antony and his queen can never have a firm love based on continuance which they reject. Unwilling to acknowledge their finiteness, both figures believe they can live above the controls of society. In the story one can find no moment of decision. From the first scene, from the first line, all is lost. The intentness toward pleasure is moving and desperate.

Auden: It's remarkable that the whole play contains only one love scene, a fact sometimes attributed to the Elizabethan condition of boy actors in female roles. Shakespeare, it is said, did not wish to risk a laughable or awkward occasion but I don't think this is the real reason. Shakespeare has little interest in the mechanics of the love situation itself; he is more interested in the phenomenon of choice. To a degree Antony chooses his death by turning, without much struggle, to Cleopatra and what she represents: the serpent, the eternal woman. When she kills herself with an asp, the reader becomes aware of another level of meaning: Cleopatra is her own death; Antony is her "poison." As long as the situation remains caught in the sexual, this must be the case. Antony dies by the sword; Cleopatra, by poison.

Griffin: According to certain historians, Cleopatra poisoned her brother, Ptolemy XIII, to whom she was married. Before her defeat she had become very interested in poisons and tried various sorts on slaves and condemned men to see which did not produce pain or convulsions. During this investigation she discovered that the asp, without causing pain, sent the victim into a gradual sleep; this was a fact she did not forget.

Auden: The use of poison is old; no one knows how old. Since medieval times it's been well-known that the gentler sex when criminally inclined—and when not?—is particularly addicted to the use of this means to remove enemies. Authorities have suggested, with considerable evidence, that women were the first to use poisoned drinks; this may be so, since it does not involve violence—

Griffin: It's secret and bloodless. Also, in the days before autopsies, it was certain and safe. It's the usual weapon in crimes of jealousy or revenge. With her milk the woman is the life-giver but she can be the death-giver as well. At the end, Cleopatra compares the snake to a babe nursed at her breast:

Charmain: O Eastern star!
Cleopatra: Peace, peace!
Dost thou not see my baby at my breast,
That sucks the nurse asleep?

Auden: Shakespeare does this to show it's all wrong.
No one in this play lacks sophistication. All qualities are
shown, except innocence; no one seems surprised or
shocked by what the others do. True, the clown is loutish
but insinuating. He heard, you remember, of a victim of the
asp, "a very honest woman but something given to lie—"
With a wry smile he wishes Cleopatra "joy of the worm"
and warns her "Give it nothing . . . it is not worth the
feeding," but his instruction goes unheeded; Cleopatra
feeds the "venomous fool" with herself. By a curious
projection, she addresses the snake as "mortal wretch."
Early in the play Cleopatra says: "Think on me, / that am
with Phoebus' amorous pinches black" and the figure,
which appears very exaggerated, justifies itself, if the
reader links it later with the image of her body turning
black from poison. The Roman soldier Dolabella becomes
compassionately interested in Cleopatra and it is he who
says, examining her body:

Here on her breast,
There is a vent of blood, and something blown;
The like is on her arm.

Griffin: Of Dolabella we know little. But it's typical of
Shakespeare that he should not have neglected the opportunity to develop a conflict even in this subsidiary character.
He is an honest, perceptive, alert young man, and he becomes real to us in the few lines given him:

Would I might never
O'ertake pursued success but I do feel,
By the rebound of yours, a grief that smites
My very heart at root.

47

The situation serves to test his loyalty and the play moves on to something else.

Auden: It's interesting to speculate why the clown calls the asp "a worm."

Griffin: It may have been the uneducated word for snake.

Auden: The whole play might be diagrammed as X devours Y. To the protagonists luxury and liquor, "that wild disguise," finally fail to conceal the truth that the world is a theater where life eats life. In the galley-scene Pompey would like to have his enemies drowned. Birds breed under the deck of Antony's ship only to be killed by birds of prey. Cleopatra destroys Antony and is destroyed by Octavius. In *Antony and Cleopatra* everything gives way to something else. The asp kills not only Cleopatra but her attendants; then, uncaught, wriggles across the fig leaves on which it marks a slimy trail. The queen who will be destroyed by worms destroys her life with one of them. Antony calls his queen a serpent and laughs. Egypt is a "cistern of scal'd snakes."

Griffin: In the first century B.C. the Egyptians practiced a special brand of erotic worship. After certain young women sacrificed their virginity to the priests they became "sacred" and had the right to give themselves, according to their caprice, to whomever they wished. Their physical passion became the token of spirituality. Whoever came to them in the name of the god might possess them and their whole purpose was to adorn and beautify love. Basically, the plot of Shakespeare's play is The Whore Transfigured. She changes at the end.

Auden: The change is not unprepared for.

Griffin: What do you think of the character Enobarbus?

Auden: It's easier to say what he's not than what he is. He's not a misogynist, though he makes hostile remarks: "Under a compelling occasion let women die." He's not a male Cassandra. Nor a cynic, nor a realist. It's true he's something of a sceptic. He has, for some time, inclined toward men. He lives in the man's bluff world of the army which has become his future. He's interested in success. To be under one leader rather than another has considerable importance for him. He tends to believe that women have no feelings. He has faith in causes. Enobarbus does not yet know that Antony, if caught between the great occasion and the woman, would not be certain what to do.

Griffin: Antony desires Cleopatra; he also desires her death, as he wished the death of Fulvia.

Auden: Enobarbus has a speech in which he imaginatively presents death in sexual terms:

> It were a pity to cast them [women] away for nothing, though between them and a great cause they should be esteemed nothing. Cleopatra, catching but the least noise of this, dies instantly: I have seen her die twenty times upon far poorer moment. I do think there is some mettle in death, which commits some loving act upon her, she hath such a celerity in dying.

Griffin: Enobarbus entertains a pretty low opinion of Cleopatra. He considers her spoiled, cowardly and incapable of dying for a moral or spiritual reason. But he does not underestimate her.

Auden: Don't forget that Shakespeare in one of the most beautiful passages makes Enobarbus speak out in convincing admiration of Cleopatra.

Griffin: To sum him up one might call Enobarbus "an armored personality"?

Auden: Yes, if you mean by that he's ignorant of what he feels. The armored personality is called, disparagingly, the smart alec, because the folk mind senses that he defeats himself. Don't forget that the wise guy starts out as the soft guy. Look at Enobarbus, who's so afraid of showing kindness which he would call "sentimentality." Protectively Enobarbus thinks: I come first, other people second. I can see what will happen. I'm not afraid. I'll seize the main chance.

Griffin: Actually, he is afraid.

Auden: Of course. Enobarbus feels anxiety because he does not know why he does things. He couldn't explain why he dislikes women, Cleopatra in particular, nor why he left Antony.

Griffin: He really does hate Cleopatra, doesn't he?

Auden: His first remark is a snide one: "Bring in the banquet quickly; wine enough / Cleopatra's health to drink." He doesn't give a damn about Cleopatra's health. He's jealous of her and jealous in a more explicitly sexual way than he could conceive. When Antony imparts the news of Fulvia's death, Enobarbus sneers: "the tears live in an onion that should water this sorrow."

Griffin: It's all tied up with the problem of feeling. He has an ideal image of himself as strong, shrewd, realistic. Potentially, he's capable of great feeling. Of course he cannot live up to this image of himself. His mind works like this: Antony is a dreamer, but thinks in practical terms. Actually, the intangible controls Enobarbus more than anyone else in the play.

Auden: It seems to him that all behavior is dictated by self-interest or self-indulgence.

Griffin: He tries to appraise the forces of the adversary, above all of Cleopatra, who in the end will defeat him. Although he calls himself humble, he has great pride. For his general, Antony, he takes the role of devil's advocate:

> I see still,
> A diminution in our captain's brain
> Restores his heart. When valor preys on reason,
> It eats the sword it fights with: I will seek
> Some way to leave him

Since Enobarbus is the cerebral type, he decides to act from calculation not feeling, and he rationalizes his way to the desertion of Antony.

Auden: Yes, it's beside the point to attribute what's happened to "a diminution in our captain's brain." Throughout the play Antony acts with passion and wholeheartedness. Enobarbus is to Antony what Aufidius was to Coriolanus: a more or less unconscious attraction exists between them. Antony—warm, open, outgoing—feels drawn to this stern man whose feelings have been repressed. Look at what happens at the scene of the final feast. Antony thanks his old servants, an act that causes Cleopatra to ask in an aside "What means this?", and Enobarbus answers: " 'Tis one of those odd tricks which sorrow shoots / Out of the mind." Enobarbus cannot cry; he has a dry heart. Later, he takes Antony to task: "What mean you, sir, / To give them this discomfort? Look, they weep." He can say this only because he does not know crying may not be a discomfort. He's one of those who just can't bear a scene: at the end he dies of a broken heart—

Griffin: —or malaria brought on by the "poisonous damp of night." He's ashamed to weep, but not to desert Antony.

Auden: Yes, he's ashamed to weep which involves feeling and not to desert Antony which, he thinks, does not involve feeling. If one used the category of the humors, he would be the choleric. Shakespeare develops the irony that the strong realistic type often proves to be ineffectual. Since Enobarbus lacks wholeheartedness, he cannot act. Cleopatra aggressively asks him: "What shall we do?", to which he answers: "Think, and die."

Griffin: In the play he has two positive acts. First, to fetch Antony when Cleopatra gives such favorable audience to Thidias. One can imagine Enobarbus' pleasure at the queen's imprudence. The second act to desert Antony.

Auden: This seems to be a very moral play. Everybody's taught something. Enobarbus learns how to feel. Consider the scene where Antony learns of the death of Fulvia. Here's Antony's reaction to the messenger who brings the news:

> There's a great spirit gone! Thus did I desire it:
> What our contempts doth often hurl from us,
> We wish it ours again; the present pleasure,
> By revolution low'ring, does become
> The opposite of itself: she's good, being gone;
> The hand could pluck her back that shov'd her on.

Thus Antony recites to himself a lesson that, later, in a different situation Enobarbus must learn. His wife to Antony is "good being gone"; Antony in turn becomes "good being gone" to Enobarbus. But once Antony is "shov'd on," Enobarbus cannot pluck him back, much as he'd like to.

Griffin: Octavius calls Enobarbus "strong"—

Auden: No, he's rigid. Masking himself in toughness, he assumes everyone is hostile and that life is a struggle of all against all. He must fight against an evil world but this is largely an externalization of the inward enemy of unaffectedness. Enobarbus never allows himself to be "naive" enough to overlook weakness in others: "But there is never a fair woman has a true face." He speaks, often, in prose. He feels a great need to excel. Whereas Cleopatra is incapable of real feeling because she has known a certain type of feeling too much, Enobarbus has inhibited his feelings so that, when Antony by one unexpected magnanimity pierces to the buried level, Enobarbus explodes.

Griffin: Quite clearly he sees "the wounded chance of Antony." When Cleopatra palters with Thidias, Enobarbus has this aside:

> Sir, sir, thou art so leaky,
> That we must leave thee to thy sinking, for
> Thy dearest quit thee.

He speaks with logic here because he unconsciously counts himself as dear to Antony as Cleopatra. When Antony generously sends his treasure and subscribes "gentle adieus and greetings," this one act undoes his false structure of expediency. Enobarbus was an honest man, but because of his alienation he must at last learn a greater discomfort than crying.

Auden: In this play a curious opposition is sustained between the two baser elements: earth and water. You recall the scene where Cleopatra goes fishing and compares the fish to Antony. Pompey can say "The sea is mine." Enobarbus tries to persuade Antony not to fight by sea. "His delights were dolphin like."

Griffin: It's interesting what a subtle person Shakespeare makes of the blunt soldier-type, Enobarbus. At first he seems to want to "earn a place in the story," he aspires to a kind of political glory but then, after he becomes chastened, he ceases to be attracted by any kind of public fame and he says, "Forgive me in thine own particular." He has become interested only in Antony's good opinion of him. At the end he achieves a purification of motive that Cleopatra, for instance, does not.

Auden: Yes. One feels no surprise that he gets along so well with Menas, the pirate.

Griffin: Many scenes have an extraordinarily sinister quality. The third scene of act four, for instance. On the eve of the battle Antony and his captains stage a drinking bout, having resolved to "drown consideration." With a sudden cinematic shift, Shakespeare takes us to the ramparts of the palace where the guards are changing. Four soldiers enter and assume foursquare positions as if the stage represented the corners of the world. They greet each other, exchange rumors, hazard conjecture in regard to the forthcoming battle and then this passage, which I would like to read, occurs:

> 3. Soldier: 'Tis a brave army,
> and full of purpose.
> *Music of the hautboys is under the stage.*
> 2. Soldier: Peace! What noise?
> 1. Soldier: List, list!
> 2. Soldier: Hark!

1. Soldier: Music i' th' air.
3. Soldier: Under the earth.
4. Soldier: It signs well, does it not?
3. Soldier: No.
1. Soldier: Peace, I say!
What should this mean?
2. Soldier: 'Tis the god Hercules, whom Antony loved,
Now leaves him.

Auden: In a very beautiful manner Shakespeare lets the
words weave back and forth from speaker to speaker. The
short, clipped words give a feeling of fear and suspense. In
this passage many emotions are caught: superstition, vague
misgiving, real doubt, mystery. Recklessly Antony and his
leaders may "drown consideration" but consideration and
reconsideration continues on the part of the common
soldiers. "'Tis the god Hercules, whom Antony lov'd, /
Now leaves him." Yes, the music comes from below but this
line makes us think of angels and unseen powers above and
around us everywhere.

Griffin: In actuality the music no doubt came from a late
street-procession in another quarter of the city . . . .

Auden: With Antony and his queen the tragic flaw exists
in a partial state; a very few have the feelings which are
tragic flaws in their pure state. The flaw, here, is less a
passion than a general attitude common to all of us almost
all the time: worldliness. This includes love of success,
popularity, love of pleasure, of art, of ourselves. The con-
verse of this is: fear of failure, of boredom, of losing one's
grip, of being on the wrong side, of being ridiculous, of
dying. If with Antony and Cleopatra the fate is more spectacular than is likely to happen to us, that's not because
they're essentially different but because they are more successful. It happens to all of us that Hercules leaves us.

Griffin: The play is, certainly, a picture of world-
catastrophe. Toward the end there's a sense of world-
annihilation, of darkness and *verdämmlichkeit*.

Auden: Let's try to analyze what happens. There is, of course, military defeat and the hopelessness of the political situation. The country will be occupied and annexed to Rome. Curiously enough, this seems relatively insignificant in comparison with the disintegration of two human beings. We are more affected by the personal defeat of Antony and Cleopatra, which has come about for quite other reasons—

Griffin: Antony and Cleopatra become more and more like Eva Braun and Hitler—

Auden: In the early part of the play Cleopatra is symbolized by water, which is associated with women, instability and fickleness. Antony, eventually, is destroyed by the water. These two persons go to pieces because of the qualities within themselves, that Shakespeare represents in various ways. In itself, theirs is not a very unusual relationship. Most of us can recall having been involved in excessive relationships with people we did not like but whom, for some reason, we could not leave—

Griffin: You can love someone you don't really like—

Auden: That's Antony and Cleopatra's dilemma. They love each other's spirit, in an essential way—

Griffin: And it's possible to like someone you don't love—

Auden: A situation much easier to cope with since it never leads to extremity. People who like each other in this way often cling closer than those who love, than those who understand. If you love someone, you can let him go.

Griffin: And the tragedy does not lie in the involvement of an excessive relationship: what is tragic is not to accept the end of that relationship.

Auden: The tragedy in this play is the refusal of suffering. The characters are committed to worldliness and sexual passion. The play might be looked on as a demonstration of Sartre's remark: "We have a body and that is very sad." The giant Antony has lost the power to grow spiritually; he believes it is no "sin to rush into the secret house of death"—

Griffin: Cleopatra, too, can no longer grow—

Auden: In order to analyze the tragic element, let us look for a bit at the historical record. In the beginning we started with a convenient classification. Given an historical situation, we said, it could be looked at in three ways: from the point of view of the realist, the romanticist, or the ironist. *Antony and Cleopatra* is closely tied in with public and private history. You can't transfer the story to anywhere except where it occurred, the world of Egypt, first century B.C. *Julius Caesar* might be put in modern dress but not this play. In *Antony and Cleopatra* even the props and costumes take on weight and importance. They are symbols of the world, and in their weight and brilliance counteract the hollowness of the human motivation. Shakespeare uses an element of irony here. In this play the human being is limited; the world, unlimited. And now let's glance at the details of the conclusion of the play.

Griffin: After the fatal sea-fight, Antony knows all is lost. Suspecting betrayal on Cleopatra's part, he wants to revenge himself against her. Fearful of his madness, Cleopatra runs for dear life to the Monument, taking along only her two attendants and the eunuch. She instructs Mardian to inform Antony that she has killed herself.

Auden: This is the story as Shakespeare tells it. As characters Antony and Cleopatra began in a certain way and have to end in a certain way. Of course, the case of Paolo and Francesca is quite different. Both stories started in history; the poetic and the popular imagination seized upon them and, after a while, made them into archetypes. Of the incident the great poet constructs a complete work of art; he files away the unnecessary and the "accidental." But the ordinary reader can learn a great deal from the actual historical situation to see what has been changed. In its own way, history can teach a man as much as art.

Griffin: I know very little about the facts of Antony's death—

Auden: He tried to kill himself by falling on his sword, but botched the job. While he was dying, his guards came in. He ordered them to carry him to Cleopatra's mausoleum, an unfinished building near the sea. It was a very hot August morning. His body was very heavy and it took them quite a long time. When they got there the great door couldn't be opened because the bolts had been shot too deep in the lock. Therefore, they placed him on the ground under Cleopatra's window. Now, the masons and builders had left some ropes hanging from the roof where they'd been working and a resourceful soldier, noticing this, suggested that Antony be placed upon a stretcher and hauled up to Cleopatra's window. This, then, was done. In the broiling sun, bothered by flies, Antony was placed on a stage and, in a few minutes, the queen and her attendants were frantically tugging and pulling at these ropes while the dying man half-conscious upon the lurching and bumping stretcher, agonized by every jolt, ascended inch by inch toward them. As he neared the window, he tried to raise himself. They managed to push and drag the wounded man, more dead than alive, through the window. Bloody and sweat-covered, they then lay him on a couch. Writhing in agony, he asked after a while for some wine and Cleopatra brought him some. He gasped out some words of advice to her: "Don't trust Octavian... trust only Proculeius," and then died. Nothing could be more different from the picture Shakespeare gives us.

Griffin: The real account has great conviction and a rather terrible quality. Of course people don't die making grand gestures and wonderful speeches—

Auden: No, what Shakespeare leaves out and what shouldn't in a way be left out is the littleness, the door that won't open, the rusty pulley, the rope that snags, the bunch of rabble about the building who talk about what's going on. They pass rumors and coarse remarks. If the queen should show up, they'd be glad to catch her and sell her to Octavius—

Griffin: It is easy for us to emotionally understand the ethic of this situation, although it is the last thing that would happen nowadays. Antony would be taken to a doctor, or to the hospital—

Auden: Yes, of course.

Griffin: The factual account gives one an added insight. That's the distinguishing characteristic of the historic: it's unimaginable. What fancy or imagination do may be impressive, but it is something else. When I read the last act of *Antony and Cleopatra*, I was moved. The poetry reaches heights that surpass anything else in the play. I felt, however, that all this had nothing to do with how people speak and act. In a violent shorthand Shakespeare was playing one character off against another, in an effort to give the reader a symbol of a rare state of mind—

Auden: I am not sure what you're trying to say—

Griffin: Art and life both have in them a tragic element. There is what has been called *le tragique quotidien*. That is, the tragic in daily life, a normal deep-rooted and penetrating element of the tragic that occurs in existence, but that has nothing to do with the so-called great adventures, sorrows and dangers.

Auden: Yes. The annals of history may have something to do with *le tragique quotidien*. We see it in the factual account of Antony's death. Their not being able to push the jammed bolts back in time. Cleopatra calling down her instructions to her attendants and their mishearing them. All this bungling and interaction of little and big has a certain tragic quality.

Griffin: Yes, history teaches one the irony in the accidental. Into the crevices of mistakes and blunders a profound meaning lodges itself.

Auden: What could be more wonderfully ironic than Octavius' speech:

The time of universal peace is near.
Prove this a prosp'rous day, the three-nooked world
Shall bear the olive freely.

Griffin: Take the three categories: the art-form, history, life; each possesses its distinctive truth. We can't dismiss what Homer said about Paris and Helen but it may be historically true the Trojan War was a conflict over trade routes in the Aegean. Pascal's remark about Cleopatra has a certain art-truth but no historical justification.

Auden: The final effect of *Antony and Cleopatra* is one of richness and power. In this play Shakespeare does not exalt the human creature, but he does exalt the world . . . . We have seen the lords of the world in undress and it's been a disillusioning sight, but they *were* lords of a great and glittering world. In this play the temptation has been the world—the real world in its splendor. Right up to the end the weather has been good; the world has been radiant; everything has shone. The Egypto-Roman world is precious—a place of delight. The key word in this play is: World. We see the glory of things as truly glorious. Even at her death the queen puts on her robes and her crown. Seen in a certain light, the world can be this way. And Shakespeare does not want us to forget it.

four

Griffin: The first thing that happens in *Coriolanus* is that we are introduced to a crowd—

Auden: Or rather a mob—that is, a passionate crowd; they are bent on getting more corn for themselves.

Griffin: Reminds me of when we mutinied in the army. We complained to the CO because the cooks kept serving us day after day very bad pancakes—we called them collision pads. The cooks had been great absolute gods to us but how frightened they became when we united and went to the captain.

Auden: The crowd is what one is added to. The members of it are addable, as distinguished from Kierkegaard's category of the Single One; that is, they have nothing in common except togetherness.

Griffin: In Coriolanus and Julius Caesar we see this distinction between the Single One and the crowd, between spirit and politics. A great leader can have a real relation to the body politic by acknowledging the legitimacy of "many-faced otherness." He knows that the men with whom he is bound up have a different way of thinking and feeling and, even in situations of conflict, his sense of justice forces him to these differences. But two particular attitudes toward the public sphere of existence stand out as negative: one, when the otherness of persons is eclipsed by the historical enthusiasm of the crowd (the feeling of closeness with a stranger in a picket line); two, when one customarily joins public opinion or the taking of a position. Here one would place the tabloid reader, the passive conformist. The individual is excused from forming an opinion or a choice, and is equipped with ones that are approved as valid.

Auden: Yes, the crowd is like a community in that it can be any size, the difference being that the We precedes the I. A mob is united by anger, lust, hate—negative feeling. What starts out as a society may through adversity of circumstance be split into a number of opposing mobs. We see this in the reports of what happened on the raft of the *Medusa*. When the raft started out from the ship, you had on it a society: 150 men with provisions with a common aim, i.e., to be towed ashore. Through particular treachery the possibility of the aim is destroyed and the lines of the raft cast off. When this happens what was a scientifically isolated society through the gradual force of hunger and pain becomes a cannibalistic group of men atomisable down to the last man. No real logical advantage unites the various groups which are formed—but rather passion and envy.

Griffin: The shipwreck in *The Tempest* illustrates a similar opposition. The civic society, as represented by Alonso, Sebastian, etc., conflicts with the social structure of the ship, the Boatswain, mariners, etc. It is a case here of the privilege of one type of power intruding upon that of another. The Boatswain complains that the passengers mar the sailors' labor; that they assist the storm. Nothing could be less important than that the passengers possess temporal power. If the King or the Duke possessed any spiritual force, that is, if they could order the elements to silence, then the sailors would yield their authority, but of course they cannot. We see, in fact, that the representatives of temporal power tend to anticipate their doom, to be self-destructive, to have "a mind to sink." But the Boatswain on the other hand retains his hope, persistence and integrity to the last, his final remark being a question, and one feels he would have asked that question up to the moment when the water rushed into his mouth. At the end the cancelling force of adversity dooms both societies but not the difference between them for Antonio and Sebastian never lose sight of the virtue of sinking with the king. Only Gonzalo—the detached, philosophic, utopian-minded individual—conceives of a power encompassed by neither the governance of the temporal leaders nor the technical skill of the sailors and invokes, without quite assenting to, "the wills above."

Auden: As we said, a crowd can be any size. But a society, i.e., people associated for a common function, has a proper size. One judges a society good or bad according to the value of its function; thus, one would declare a labor union, say, to be better than a moonlight requisitioning detail. Insofar as a family is a responsible unit one would give it moral precedence over a counterfeiting ring. One makes a distinction between a pirate gang and an army, the distinction being less of function—looting occurs in both—than of proper size, for it is clear that a pirate gang represents an accidentally cumulative group; conquered crews of any size are impounded. What distinguishes piracy from military maneuvers is that it is a going on and on, a haphazard depredation, not a strategic scheme wherein unit is weighed against unit. . . . In *Coriolanus* Shakespeare emphasizes that a crowd forms a dangerous vacuum; he represents its inconstancy. It starts out by hating the Single One, swerves to idolizing him, then back to hate at the end. A mob is a pseudosociety in that it may set out to do something—

Griffin: To lynch a man, for instance—

Auden: Yes. A mob may be composed of all classes. Recently I read a write-up of that lynching in Greenville, Mississippi. When one of the participants, the scion of a good local family, was interrogated, he answered: "I just went along with the others because they were doing it," which in a sense seems worse than saying "I wanted to kill a man."

Griffin: That is, a mob involves an automatism of act in which you pattern your behavior on the man in front of you.

If isolated in a special group one may find this power of mimicry a great advantage—in the army, for instance—

Auden: Unless completely demoralized by victory or defeat, most army units cannot be equated with mobs; their training forbids that. A mob must be fused by strong emotion, say, a will to destroy. Little of this desire to destroy exists in soldiers because of a failure of faith. In politics the one who arouses feeling in the public will triumph over whoever tries to curtail feeling on the same platform. What is the first qualification of a crowd master? To arouse emotions in others with no compulsion to feel them. "Disingenuous compliances," as Dr. Johnson called them. Brutus is shocked when he sees Caesar working the tricks. The fickleness of the people, the fact that those less worthy than himself may gain their approval, these things offend Coriolanus. In dealing with the acts of the soldiers Shakespeare delineates crowd behavior. In Act I, Scene v, when the soldiers are engaged in looting, scorned by their leader, and in Act I, Scene iv, when the two soldiers are betting, they have become crowd-members united by greed and by accident respectively. The latter incident is particularly wonderful when in order to break the monotony the soldiers would be glad to bet against their own interest. Menenius and Volumnia both believe in "disingenuous compliances." Menenius is something of a Machiavellian conservative. Ruled by prudence he would say that the best course is to know the right people, to be decently dishonest.

Griffin: This, too, is not a matter of rank, is it? Privates, captains, generals, all believe in the sanctity of chance and the honor of loot?

Auden: Surely. Marcius makes a great show of contempt for the pillaging Romans but a few lines on, when Lartius offers to help him, says,

The blood I drop is rather physical
Than dangerous to me; to Aufidius thus
I will appear, and fight.

A statement which seems obvious vanity, an ostentation. What remains important is that his rival should see him at a dramatic moment. And Lartius gradiloquently invokes the "fair goddess Fortune."

Griffin: Clausewitz has a passage where he philosophizes on the element of accident in war. He says,

> Three-fourths of the things on which action in war is based lie hidden in the fog of a greater or less obscurity. In no other sphere of human activity has such a margin to be left to chance, because none is in such constant contact with it on every side. Owing to this fortuity of all reports and assumptions, the person acting in war always finds things different from his expectations.

Auden: Looting is a sexual makeshift. The object becomes a substitute for virginity, for the unique love.

Griffin: To return to the passage you mentioned: Marcius, as you say, makes a show of contempt for the thieving Romans but then in the same speech cries: "And hark, what noise the general makes! To him! / There is the man of my soul's hate, Aufidius. . . ." He might just as well say "of my soul's love," so clearly these interconnect here. Tabus against the gentler emotion force him to repress, and the feeling comes out in the socially acknowledged form of magnetic antagonism as strong in one case as in the other. This pattern appears clearly in adolescent sports. The whole play in fact might be called a history of a repression—with intermittent lapses. For Coriolanus' spectacular dislike is a defense system, a reaction formation erected against his feeling for Aufidius, and the desire to meet him in hand-to-hand combat forms, as did the duels of German students, a distorted proof of affection. In the end Coriolanus subordinates himself to his mother and wife, i.e., in order to free himself from men he subjugates himself to women. . . . When I was in Japan I saw that the black market between GI and Japanese had a sexual element in it. Nothing could have been more like the encounter between prostitute and client—the unrest, consultations, uncertainties, brevity. One side was covertly anxious to sell and the other secretly eager to buy—hence the mock play. Between the poles of hesitation the transaction occurred with an essential fleecing. Afterward both parties desired to part as soon as possible being conscious of the overlying threat. Like all men, soldiers desire to be loved—to be loved for themselves alone. The object they procure through barter—a fan, obi or bit of metal—becomes for them the symbol of a unique love.

I remember a conversation I had with my friend Mac about the prostitutes. Our contacts occurred not with real geishas, these being reserved for officers, but rather with ex-factory workers or middle-class mompei-girls in communal houses, but a few of them had had some sort of aesthetic training. Often it was necessary to wait a long time in line and you were rushed through; but at other houses this was not so, and Mac would say, "It is wonderful. They're very polite, they sing to you—play a guitar or dance a little for you." Above all, this was important to him. Why? He wanted, I think, to believe he was being made an exception of, that is, whatever song they sang they did for him alone. It became a performance which like all aesthetic acts differed—though slightly—from any other performance. The sex act might become mechanical, the aesthetic act could not. Further, the commercial sex act exists with its cancellation (the prophylactic), but for the aesthetic, which in a sense may be more dangerous, there is no prophylactic. . . .

Auden: I've sometimes wondered why men pay women for this. Pride, contempt, hostility and need, these emotions go into the man's giving his body to the woman and paying money, which is an excretory symbol, for hers. As Baudelaire remarked, "There are only two places where one pays for the right to spend: women and public latrines." Some people conceive of prostitution in peacetime as a safeguard for marriage; there's some truth in this. In former societies men possessed most of the money; they set up factories, monopolies, cartels, etc. The house of ill fame may be looked on as a corporation to satisfy the sexual consumer—typically a man because of his aggressivity. But if women get hold of the money, as they seem to be doing, they might be able to do away with prostitution. The verb meaning to have intercourse used in the denigrative sense of outwitting or defeating comes from the conviction of male sex superiority. And the reproductive act has sometimes been compared to the occupation of one person by another, hence to the relation of a conqueror and a conquered thing. Everyone knows that erotic male talk has a close connection with military terms. The man gives himself *and* the money to the prostitute whereat he goes back to his wife then repeating the process which seems to be a reflex action. Both acts may be a desperate search for an inaccessible type of emotion.

Griffin: A house of prostitution composes a society.

Auden: Yes. The two great drives are food and greed. For the prostitute sex instead of being a way of love becomes a form of work. To her client sex instead of being a way of love becomes a hunger where the girls are treated as food. In a brothel you have equity and consent; one want is exchanged for another. The idea of the brothel exceeds class and convention, and the law has no power to deal with it. The brothel manager depends on people committing fornication. A society is a group of people associated in terms of a common function. A brothel is a society. Their function is fornication. Pompey in *Measure for Measure* says, "I do find your hangman is a more penitent trade / than your bawd; he doth oftener ask for forgiveness."

Griffin: We started out by talking of different forms of togetherness. *Coriolanus* begins with the activity of an armed mob; *Julius Caesar* with a minor conflict between classes.

Auden: Historically we have two definitions of society. Cicero's: A society is a group of people associated by common advantage and common right. St. Augustine's definition:

A society is a group of rational beings united by a common function. The first will not hold water. If joined by a common advantage, men cannot be joined by a common sense of right.

Griffin: Even the commoners in Shakespeare often seem to have great stature. In the very first scene of *Coriolanus* the ordinary people act rather magnificently, particularly the First Citizen. If we looked around today I don't know where we would find the like. In the microcosm-macrocosm dialogue, the First Citizen really stands up to Menenius. The former's faults are precipitancy and contempt: "Why stay we prating here? To th' Capitol!" A nice touch here because these, too, are the defects of his enemy, Caius Marcius. Shakespeare does not represent the people as very bad. The reader must distinguish between how they act and how their despisers accuse them of acting.

Auden: Yes. If you went to Union Square to find your modern "First Citizen," you'd see plenty of dissatisfied "radicals" but none with the integrity or talent for action of Shakespeare's Citizen. Talking to them a little you'd discover in them all divisive ideologies: one would be a pacifist, another a Stalinist, a Shackmanite, an anarchist, etc. Commonly at odds with the social order they would be unable to envisage any common scheme of political action. In *Coriolanus* the First Citizen might be called a Leninist and Menenius a gradualist.

Griffin: Since so many types of togetherness are dealt with here—the family, city, army, crowd, etc.—often these blocs come in subtle conflict as when Shakespeare causes Volumnia to say after her son's exile, "Now the red pestilence strike all trades in Rome, / And occupations perish!" She has more regard for her son than for a whole city. Again and again Shakespeare turns his attention to the disparity between the personal and the political motive. Investigation into particular cases seems to prove that the virtuous man is never quite powerless nor the powerful man wholly vicious.

Often the tragedy of a historical situation is that a regular guy achieves a position of power ignorant of how to use his potentiality for good, e.g., Lorenzo de Medici. Coriolanus is a person obsessed by the idea of self-transcendence. Quite disinterested he does not want to seem better than the others; he wants *to be* better. He seeks continual realization of himself in deeds. Innocent of a bent for politics he cannot manipulate the crowd or bring himself to use his power, yet his mother pushes him into a quasi-political position.

Auden: Coriolanus does not become the member of any community; his ties remain negative. Toward the end he tries, as Jesus did, to divorce himself from his family. A word that casts reflection on him will send him in a rage. When Volumnia pleads with him to spare Rome, her reasoning has no effect; not till she scolds does he relent. One sees that he requires of the people a relation where he is the only child. Volumnia wants by proxy to be a politician, a savior— the common people call her "mad." Her son has a passion to surpass others; he can rule the crowd but has no talent for dealing with the individual. A little incident brings this out. After being lavishly praised by his general, he desires only that Cominius free a poor captive but he cannot recall his name. He is lost when he has to deal with a particular case. In his thought Volumnia and Aufidius compete; he both hates and loves them. A terrific emulation animates Aufidius although he presents it to himself as hate. Caius Marcius would like to establish a special relation with him and all his exploits are an effort to attract. After his encounter with his friend-enemy he asks for wine; he retreats into narcosis. To explain his going over to the other side as merely a cold heartless thirst for revenge against his country seems to me a misreading. The irony lies much deeper. It consists in what Cooley called "the sympathy of percussion." That is, a curious bond exists between the heads of opposing forces—a greater closeness than between generals and those under them. This point of behavior fascinated Shakespeare and in *Troilus and Cressida* he made Achilles say,

> I'll... invite Trojan lords after the combat
> To see us here unarmed. I have a woman's longing,
> An appetite that I am sick withal,
> To see great Hector in his weeds of peace,
> To talk with him and to behold his visage,
> Even to my full of view.

Griffin: Back in 1945 *Newsweek* printed some frank remarks made by Field Marshal Montgomery. He commented to a reporter, "Rundstedt is the best German general I have come up against in the war. He knows his stuff. I would very much like to get myself into Rundstedt's brain for a couple of minutes. I have a picture of him in my room. I wanted a picture of Rundstedt very badly." And we see that Achilles wanted *to talk to* Hector, that is, to establish a social relation, to break through the autopathic pattern which he finds imposed upon them both.

Auden: But in the case of Caius Marcius [Coriolanus] it is something deeper. It proceeds not only from an equality of grandeur but from suppressed desire. His first remarks to his military superior concern Aufidius: "He is a lion / That I am proud to hunt."

At close intervals this motif is emphasized throughout the play. In Scene vi he begs his general to set him against his great rival. After his consulship he desires to oppose Aufidius' hatred fully. Coriolanus' grand speech before his opponent's house in Antium beginning "O world, thy slippery turns!" forms an explosive refutation of the accepted "enemy-fallacy" of war. The ensuing scene of impassioned reconciliation abounds in details of attraction and repulsion particularly where Aufidius projects in phantasy the nature of their hand-to-hand combat. The attitude of Coriolanus has less envy in it than Aufidius', but upon their encounter the latter's jealousy subsides in the warmth of the immediate response. Each is fascinated by the other's genius in war and nobility of command. Since Coriolanus' valor is greater, he begins to attract those under Aufidius and to darken the latter. Aufidius and his rival are constructed of a more heroic mold than Menenius, Cominius or Titus. What Aufidius resents above all is that,

> At a few drops of women's rheum which are
> As cheap as lies, he sold the blood and labor
> Of our great action.

A similar love-tension exists between Caesar and Brutus but in this case the former's death is brought about with far less inevitability. It seems less inherent in Caesar's nature and more of a palace intrigue.

Griffin: What Aufidius resents is not the slaughter Caius Marcius created in Carioli nor the fact that he has been beaten by him. What he essentially cannot bear is that Coriolanus should allow a woman to come between them, the only woman with the stature to be his rival, his friend's mother. I agree with you that step by step Coriolanus' death is brought about with greater inevitability. Coriolanus is death-driven. His encounter with Aufidius climaxes his search for the death situation. After this proves not to be it, Coriolanus has to push things to an extreme, for he seeks to die at the significant not the easy time. Although unchastened by experience, Coriolanus has a vision of what life should be. Because he has this over-rectitude about life, he will not compromise with those who have no sense of potentiality. He attempts to stand "as if a man were author of himself and knew no other kin." Utterly self-centered he cannot become a class leader or a master of destiny. People like him, spoiled by fortune and inheritance, those who appear often as rulers are usually least able to rule themselves. The well-integrated, modest individual knows that by merely existing with others he has obligations to them; Coriolanus acknowledges none to anyone but himself.

Auden: A smooth-running body politic is constantly

threatened by men like Coriolanus or Caesar, those who through their gifts demand greater importance than allowable for the proper running of society. This play forms a diagram of the relation between the Many, the Few and the One. All governments have been essentially oligarchical. Roughly you have two larger strata: the middle class from whom the crowd master arises and the unleavened dough of humanity—in this play the fickle citizens, whether Romans or Volscians—who remain politically unaware, who cannot rule or suffer to be ruled and in the end will bring about the ruin of the One. The small top stratum consists of the elite (here, Menenius, Cominius and Coriolanus, etc.) who, having with difficulty attained power, are bent on retaining it. Their life remains a constant struggle with the Few, the Tribunes, the cleverer members of the middle class aware of the precarious position of their rulers. The social student conceives of all sizable wars as conflicts projected either by the elite in order to divert the plebeians or by the middle class in an attempt to dislodge the power of the patricians and enthrone themselves as an elite to be eventually dislodged. If we reflect on this we'll see that for some reason the elite must be guilty of a fatal flaw. Many have assumed that defect to be the corruptibility inherent in the holding of power. "Power corrupts. . . ."

Griffin: But surely political power differs radically from other forms of power. By his skill and judgment a surgeon holds decisive power over the lives of others; the objectivity of his profession prevents him from being spoiled by this. William Penn possessed absolute power over the lives and destinies of the colonists who came with him on the *Welcome*; however, he didn't abuse that power.

Auden: Because of the gap between the public, the undifferentiated mass, and the instrumentalities of government, a great deal of deception exists in politics. This cannot be called the fault of any strict group whether in the top elite, the *juste milieu* or the bottom. The inside of politics never edifies. And democratic politicians are not much better than aristocratic or totalitarian ones. Because the talents a politician uses are not disinterested, creative or even specialized, there is something to be said for the small libertarian community which would be arranged to allow each man in turn to govern the whole settlement for a short period of time. Political jurisdiction would become like jury duty. I think this would be likely to turn out better than the rigid guardianship Plato recommended without convincing us how the potential guardians could be justly chosen.

Griffin: Since, then, the elite usually misuses its power till the lower strata become so indignant that they revolt, in turn seize power and become equally unjust and bureaucratic, isn't the problem to find how the powerful may become virtuous and those who are virtuous be given political influence?

Auden: Yes, it is curious that most of the wise and good men have shunned temporal power—Socrates, Jesus, Lao-tse, etc. Plato was given the opportunity to train the young ruler Dionysius but the effort turned out badly. Yet temporal power has nothing in it which need contaminate a good person. The circulation of the elite is due not only to the chicanery of politics but to the laziness of the Great Aggregate and the lack of ethics in collective behavior. Acting in groups seems to be characterized by a special psychology that includes mimicry, loss of initiative and parliamentary self-entanglement. As everyone knows, committees are efficient in wasting the individual's time.

Griffin: To go back to this play. May one not say, then, that Coriolanus' chief flaw is his ignorance of the Augustinian City of God?

Auden: Yes. It is not that he does not try to be fair; he does. He is not greedy for gain. Though he refuses to distribute corn gratis among the rioting crowd, still he would not oppress the people. He would reject tyrannical power and posts of self-advancement. However, he has no inkling of that ethical city which cuts across class lines, the divine charter of which may sometimes be found in the poorest and most uneducated breast. As Aufidius says,

> So our virtues
> Lie in th' interpretation of the time;
> And power, unto itself most commendable,
> Hath not a tomb so evident as a chair
> T' extol what it hath done.

If it be fluent and molded to the circumstances of the time, power may not be evil. One individual will show greater skill in one field than another. Naturally he will rise to the top and attain power in his particular sphere. Occasionally you have a universal man like da Vinci or Goethe. God intends to show us that power in one sphere need not shut out achievement in others. A king can be a philosopher. A scientist, a good man. A politician, a poet. The only type of community which can be hoped for now is that of many-sided individuals of this sort.

Griffin: Today that sort of man must stand alone.

Auden: Largely so. The dilemma is made very clear by Buber, who states that it may be right for a believing man to join a group but belonging to it he must remain submissive also to a higher authority. His decision will thus at times oppose a tactical decision of the group. Knowing the truth brought forth by his conscience, he will carry this forward into the group itself, thereby establishing an inner front in it. This can be more important, as Buber remarks, than all fronts drawn today between groups, for this front, if it is upright and honest, may run as a secret unity across all groups. At times this type of person may succumb to the temptation of believing himself helpless.

Griffin: We have in *Coriolanus* a blueprint of the relations between the One, and the Few and the Many. The latter are interested in corn, games; some say they want war; some, peace without any clear idea of what they mean. Cowardly,

73

greedy, swayed by public speeches, they form a crowd, and the characteristic of a crowd is its lack of memory. The present moment seems absolute to it. What is depicted in *Coriolanus* happened in Germany. When you talked to the postwar Germans, they earnestly claimed they were against Hitler, were forced to do what they did, etc.; and I do not think they were conscious of lying. After what had happened, the great destruction, the collapse of the social order, all that remained in their minds was the sense of the moment; they had no memory. Of course, such conduct is not confined to one nationality. Most of us are members of the crowd, if we are not careful. The crowd envelops any of us when we are not a part of a society with a common function or of a community with a common love. What would you give as an example of a good society?

Auden: A jam session. There the number of instruments and the improvisatory element are important. If a society cannot exercise improvisation (creative politics) it dies. When its function is discharged, the society should be dissolved. Because of the self-perpetuating nature of certain societies (e.g., the two-party system in this country) we run into difficulty. When its function is permanent (world government) the individuals must be replaced by others. If a society insists on continuing when its function has been outlived, it becomes comic or dangerous. If it freezes into a habit without communication it becomes funny (the bridge party). If it expands beyond its need, it becomes dangerous (an army in peacetime). Volumnia becomes a peril when she tries to regard a grown-up as a child to educate. If the society disbars those with the same qualifications, it threatens itself. Also, it will decline if it includes those who do not share its aims.

Griffin: How careful Plato was about this! All who qualified intellectually—men and women, workmen and patricians—composed the society of the guardians. Above all, they must show an identification with the society and a willingness to live up to their obligations.—How does the society differ from the community?

Auden: A community is a group of rational beings associated on the basis of a common love. By having no fixed size it may endanger itself. Externally it is threatened by two things: one, the crowd because they have no stabilizing desire or consciousness of self; two, the individual or group wanting a special place of admiration.

Griffin: At last human beings have reached the point where they can form small federations. The ordinary soldiers in one army may feel sympathy for their comrades-in-arms but most of them lack the imagination to sympathize with those in the enemy force, yet they are precisely the ones who are undergoing the same experiences themselves. Men have got to the point where they can bring together national bodies that are dangerous but they cannot seem to make the leap which would allow them to ally themselves with those of different races, educations and religions.

Auden: Both communities and societies are more easily, though less strongly, established negatively, i.e., by a shared fear of the external than by a shared love. At the end of the play their fear of Coriolanus unites the Romans more cohesively than any sense of previous community could do.... A community is something one joins. Unlike the society it has no definite size. The optimum size of a community is infinity if what its members love is good. But if what they love is bad, the optimum size is zero. The crowd, unlike the society, has no common function. It develops under these conditions: when an individual cannot find his unique place. That is, where there is unemployment or in any mass production society that uses the individual as a mere labor unit. The crowd amalgamates when communities disappear and individuals cease to love anything. It takes place when men lose the ability to choose between true alternatives and when they lose faith in aesthetic values. With great art Shakespeare fills *Coriolanus* with the cries of crowds, with the sounds of public life. The author uses a great profusion of public music—drums, trumpets, flourishes of cornets, oboes, sennets—as well as the sounds of public intercourse which form a kind of music—bustle, riots, parleyings, alarums, the friction of togetherness. Of course, the characters probably don't know one note from another. . . .

five

Griffin: My friend Arnold Jaffe is an anarchist of a peculiar brand. He will not ask directions of a policeman; he lives in a cellar on herbs and roots; he writes letters to the *Times*, and strangely enough a while ago he fell in love with a woman detective.

Auden: Thus bright things come to confusion.

Griffin: Naturally his love for Marjorie, that is the detective's name, immediately began to conflict with some of his most cherished beliefs. She wants him to marry her but Jaffe does not believe in the ceremony of marriage. However, emotionally he desires to marry her because he senses that she'll leave him if he doesn't. It'll be interesting to see what happens—

Auden: The anarchist is the defiant rebel who usually lacks creativity; he is the human being transfixed into the pillar constantly looking back at the smoke, fire and destruction of society. There is in him too the wild prophet who takes his place in the forum; he can preach his beard off but people will pay no attention, and then he tends to look down his nose at the people. Secretly he's a little disturbed because of the discrepancy between his words and acts.

Griffin: To what, do you think, is that discrepancy due?

Auden: The anarchist finds himself faced with the choice of inhibiting his acts or toning down his theory so that it lacks daring. This means he must set up for himself ideals, not a bad thing, if he knows that the dream is a dream and that he must suffer for it. At least the anarchist feels something; he's sure of that. And he remains unimpressed by the word-juggling around us everywhere. He is not tyrannized over by language.

Griffiin: D.H. Lawrence, for instance, was strong on feeling. From the very first, he resisted the bombardment of war propaganda. Would you, I wonder, call him an anarchist?

Auden: Lawrence's case is curious. We see from books like *The Plumed Serpent* that he believed in what one might call a soft primitivism. That is, he drew the contrast between the dark gods of the blood and the reflective mental consciousness; he created a version of Rousseau's "noble savage," the instinctive man who acts naturally. This soft primitivism is, I think, dangerous in that it usually results not in a form of conservatism but nihilism, a we-are-all-sunk feeling. We had better withdraw. As far as possible Lawrence wanted to stand outside his time. The war came as a great shock to him; he felt a certain disgust with England and began to think in terms of the possibility of going with a few choice friends to America where he could establish a free community around himself. He said to his friends: "Let's stay clean. Let's not try to do anything with the world any more. The world is extinguished, bent on destroying itself. The only hope now is to get away—far away somewhere and try to be happy because I believe the goal of the individual is to be happy." He thought he'd have a better chance of being happy in a primitive community. The people he saw around him in wartime London made him sick. Lawrence came from an industrialized community and all his life was trying to escape into a more primitive society where he'd be more likely, he thought, to find a community of instinctive people. He, of course, never found this but he never gave up "shopping around."

Griffin: He did feel that the Pueblo Indians were happier than the American tourists in Taos, that on the whole they behaved better, led more satisfactory, solider lives.

Auden: Yes, but one can't call Lawrence an anarchist, as the word is generally understood. World War I was a shock to him but not as great a shock as World War II was to Virginia Woolf. I remember that Virginia Woolf makes her heroine, Mrs. Ramsay, think: there's no treachery too base for the world to commit; but Mrs. Woolf herself never really thought that.—At different times in his life Lawrence was more utopian in his approach to these problems than at others. He was rather anarchistic in that he clung to A Purpose which he thought of as outside himself. One finds so many contradictions in his life. Sprung from the working class he had, I think, a naive awe for the higher born—look at his relations with The Honorable Dorothy Brett, Lady Ottoline Morrell and Lady Asquith. But he was not a snob—

Griffin: No. In a sense, you might call him a born aristocrat. He had no hereditary title but instead a title of intellect, of feeling, that gave him a nobility. Lawrence knew his own value and so did most people who met him. He was a naturally distinctive person. It is curious that the English believe in the principle of noblesse oblige, but they have a largeness of feeling about nobility too. One can inherit the title of duke or lord. Another person from any class can become, in an existential sense, a duke, a lord. I think Disraeli is a case in point.

Auden: Lawrence was a solipsist. He believed that his self was the only reality. In his beast poems he does not think of the beast as outside himself, he becomes the beast. To a person of this type all reality takes on an intensely subjective aspect: you remember his feeling for Susan and his anger at the killing of the porcupine, a noble sincere anger—very rare in this age. Lawrence really had what Schweitzer called "reverence for life."

Griffin: Fortunately Schweitzer succeeded in detaching himself from civilization; he returned to the primitive and found a way to coordinate preachment and practice.

Auden: Lawrence could have done that. But he had less trouble in separating himself from the zones of civilization than from his women disciples with whom he never got along and whom he did not like. He never found adequate human material to implement his fine ideas.

Griffin: Yes. He once made this revealing remark, "You know I was not meant to be primarily a writer."

Auden: He had a great hunger for mastery. Because he had always to overrule, he surrounded himself with second-rate people; they made him feel safe. Bertrand Russell, Katherine Mansfield and others who were his equals he fought with and separated from. On meeting Lawrence one would first of all have to clear the stage of domination. Right away one should say "Oh you *dreary* consumptive. You're not so hot. Shut up. I'll live longer than you will." After that you'd get along with him famously.

Griffin: He was never able to dominate Frieda—

Auden: That's why he stuck to her. She talked back.

Griffin: You said, a while back, that Lawrence was no snob. How do you define a snob?

Auden: He's a man who's motivated by misguided self-interest. Proust himself was not a snob but his character of Mme. Verdurin was a culture-snob.

Griffin: Proust was a social climber, an outsider—

Auden: Oh yes, that gave him his detachment and penetration but he was not a snob; he had too much humanity. And one sees by his treatment of the Duchesse de Guermantes that he felt no excessive vulgar regard for wealth and social standing in themselves.

Griffin: Thackeray says a snob is one who meanly admires mean things.

Auden: Yes, and Proust's discovery of his vocation had put him outside all that. Thackeray's definition is rather harsh. As part of his poetic endowment Proust felt great enthusiasm for the names of French nobility; this does not make him a snob. As a writer he had broader sympathies than Virginia Woolf, for instance. Look at his presentation of Françoise and the footman who quotes Lamartine. Lemaître described a snob as "a sheep who follows the leader with a conceited air."

Griffin: For these things the French have an exact regard. The French and the American snob desire different things: the Frenchman to be the first of his class whatever it may be but the American to stand last in the first class of society. Would you call a friend I'll refer to as "Dominic Straightly" a snob?

Auden: He is, I think, a person primarily interested in power. He's not a young man with malice or meanness; he's an opportunist, not a snob. He has, of course, talent, but his idea of success has gotten thoroughly mixed up with his concept of good writing. In order not to destroy, ambition must be mixed with love. Dominic has the morbid desire to rise in the world untempered by a desire for the esteem of his fellow man; the hard wish to succeed—not shine, not serve—succeed, and he desires this, why?—because already the world and his fellow man have galled him. Dominic, you see, regards success as important (which it isn't, though publication is); he therefore spends most of his time getting on top rather than concentrating on writing well, which is hard enough to take all his time. The chief characteristic of the opportunist is that he's sunk in the immediate; he cannot see ahead.

Griffin: Would you say an opportunist may be a man of principle?

Auden: Yes. However, he defeats himself. Since he can't truly look ahead and gauge probabilities, he cannot be sure what will be to his advantage. Pascal said, "We know ourselves so little that many think they are well when they are near death, unconscious of approaching fever, or of the abscess ready to form itself."

Griffin: In America particularly the young man from the provinces, the Lucien de Rubempré, the Dominic Straightly who's fashioned for himself an image of success seems to have become a common phenomenon.

Auden: Yes. These people are apt to be naive... and ruthless. The Dominic Straightly is a person who has said from the start, "I want to be a writer." Irresponsibly he has looked ahead and glimpsed a concept of the writer that has pleased his ego; has glimpsed the position of the writer (or rather what he conceives it to be) with privileges and rewards; he is, however, usually unwilling to go through the hard intermediate stages of study. That's why such a person says, "I want *to be a writer*," not "I want to write." That is, he has not fallen in love with the possibility of a specific work he's compelled to do. You remember in the old stories and in *The Magic Flute* the hero must fall in love with the princess or the idea of a princess before he has actually seen her and, when he starts out for her, he must undergo different trials, by water or fire, for the suffering itself eventually creates the princess. The Dominic Straightly phenomenon is the logical upshot, I think, of the materialistic expansion here beginning around the end of the Civil War.

Griffin: A person like Dominic is fascinated by what he calls "the great world"; it has for him an aesthetic beauty and attraction.

Auden: There's nothing wrong in that. Henry James adored "the great world." So did Proust, in a way. But you can see how Dominic's attitude differs from Proust's. Until 1913 Proust's real creative, as apart from his journalistic, life remained to most of his associates a secret. To the comtesses and princesses he was "little Marcel," a good end man for a party. However, although most of his friends thought of him as a *flâneur*, he continued to lead a hidden life. The Dominic Straightly today acts differently. First of all he possesses no secret life.

Griffin: Both the Dominic Straightly and the Proust must have a solid private income.

Auden: Around the twenties a new romantic attitude had formed in regard to money. Take the case of Scott Fitzgerald. In a naive way Fitzgerald romanticized money; his wife required it (safer in the long run). But this did not work to Fitzgerald's advantage as a writer. With all his endowment he should have written a great deal more, good as what he did write was. His feeling—for it was a feeling—about money is curious; he thought it made a man freer; that it made him more interesting. Of course money in itself has nothing to do with the phenomenon of freedom or choice. Money can enlarge the material area in which a free agent can choose but it can't make him choose well or badly. It can, in fact, only hedge him with complication and obstruction. Since the artist's product is unique, it has no standard economic value. If a poet produces two poems that does not necessarily double his paycheck. Since its origin is mysterious and outside time, the work of the artist cannot be translated into constant financial terms; this is a curse and a boon. Artists can flatter for money because they need to take what they can in that way. But an artist cannot demand praise *and* money for his work. In a bureaucracy such as this an artist has to be a mixture of the child and the Machiavellian. He must be prudent as Prince Hal; he must have the wisdom of doves and serpents. In a complex society one of the things he must do is know the right people; he must be "decently dishonest" as Mr. Rockefeller said. The Dominic Straightly has learned this type of shrewdness; that's about all he has learned.

Griffin: He has no profound secret life to which he can turn?

Auden: You see the difference. In Proust's case he wore a mask. Right up until 1907 he went to all the chic gatherings; talked amusingly; got his material. To the dinner party people, his other life remained unknown. But in the case of the Dominic Straightlys they talk flippantly and their acts seem to confirm what they say. They are, or become, their flippancy. Sooner or later this destroys the human element in their life and work.

Griffin: What do you think of *Remembrance of Things Past*?

Auden: It's a great novel. But Proust, like Wilde, never got past the aesthetic stage of religion. *The Past Recaptured* is a frightening book because all those people, not excepting the I, are in Hell and don't know it.

Griffin: To go back, for a moment, to what we talked about at the beginning: the discrepancy, in connection with the anarchist, between preachment and deed. Don't you find that same discrepancy in the case of the artist?

Auden: Oh yes. You find it in the case of everyone except the saint. The artist, like Proust, may make a religion of his art. But the saint is immersed in life; each of his acts is, itself, a religious observance. That's the difference between a Keats, say, and a Schweitzer.

Griffin: Yes.

Auden: Schweitzer is, in his way, a saint, and a less cranky one than some. All saints are cranky, even the most wonderful; the reverse of course, is not true. One should be very careful to distinguish between the saint and the hysteric; the saint is *totally there*; the hysteric is brilliant and charming. At a certain point eccentricity in art and ethic becomes unjustifiable. The difficulty is to determine that point, particularly in regard to behavior. Take a concrete situation. When a beggar asks for money, I'll give him some change if I have it, but should he buttonhole me with a long story, I'll regard it as phony; it's got nothing to do with his need or desire for money; it represents a neurotic need—the need to be listened to, which is common in this society and makes the psychoanalysts lots of money. Be careful never to give disproportionately. If a beggar asks for a quarter, don't give him $5. That only dislocates the balance, emphasizing the economic space between you and him; he'll then let his imagination go wild and be angry because you didn't give more.

Griffin: What about the claim that almsgiving perpetuates the status quo?

Auden: In back of that lies a monstrous attitude. I'm horrified by people who say, "Don't be kind to servants and workers, then they'll be more likely to revolt!" If I'm accused of perpetuating the status quo, I answer: All right. How the status quo can be changed I haven't discovered yet; I'm sure the way wouldn't be by refraining from giving. To be unkind for political reasons or in order to make a group class-conscious involves a confusion of the personal and the political.

Griffin: In a crude way panhandlers act as an abrasive on a sick society. More than the rest they make society "work" for them without cooperating with its evils. They are not completely defeated victims of a social psychology of success as the Straightlys are the victims of an aesthetic psychology of success.

Auden: Yes, except that you can't talk about the "evils of society." Per se a social structure is not good or bad. The individual and the social cadre constantly interact. The first attack on the problem must be from within his consciousness. And that's very difficult.

Griffin: Yes, for the means of propaganda have gotten to be the climate of all our lives.

Auden: One good method of resistance against the police state is incorrectly filling out forms. Supply inaccurate information to the questions so dear to them. When they have the impertinence to demand your religion, answer "Druid" or "Lemurian." That'll cause weeks of research and, with any luck, your papers'll get lost. Several of my friends in Germany escaped being put in ovens this way. Many involved forms were sent them; they tore them up; official-dom is more easily confounded by utter evasion than anything else.

Griffin: Once you have anything to do with the wheels, the wheels start turning; you're sunk.

Auden: Yes, the police chief has the power of a small dictator and he prides himself on being unillusioned about human nature. He has none of the idealism of the political dictator. The latter takes the trouble to throw a veil of messianism over his acts; he's really interested in inventing a

85

myth. Totalitarianism starts out as a shortcut to a golden age; it ends in malice and destruction. The tyrant is usually a moralist manqué. Saint-John Perse once told me a story which illustrates this. . . . Things were going bad for Italy, so Mussolini arranged to meet Briand at Trieste. Briand and Perse were kept waiting for a long time in a marble lobby surrounded by muscular statues and gilt scrollwork. At the end of the hall, finally, two gaudily uniformed henchmen flung aside a huge door. Then Mussolini strode down a great red carpet. In full regalia he approached Briand, clicked his heels, stiffly bowed, then pushed him into a tiny bare anteroom. As soon as they were alone, all Mussolini's grandioseness fell away. In a confidential manner they chatted. Il Duce seemed earnest and quiet. Suddenly he turned to Briand and asked: "What can I do to become respectable?" Briand glanced at him coldly. "It's too late," he said.

six

Griffin: Do you think that the young man of the *Sonnets* was an actor?

Auden: Yes, and since Shakespeare himself was one, you get a great deal of dramatic psychology in the poems. You remember in many of the poems Shakespeare urged W. H. to marry—

Griffin: He was disturbed by a particular type of adolescent beauty that is very transitory and that represented for him a symbol of the beauty of the moment—the thing that must be rescued from time.

Auden: Since that type of beauty is unrelated to function, a good-looking man is a biologic luxury from a sexual point of view. Shakespeare chides W. H. for his celibacy; he compares his single state to an image in a mirror—

Griffin: And to a self-fed flame, a sum of money spent upon itself, a ruined roof—

Auden: But the mirror image has particular significance. To Shakespeare W. H. stands for change.... Of course, in those days boys assumed women's parts often to great effect for, since they were able to do so for only a few years, this volatility added a kind of pathos to the performance and compelled a healthy detachment on the part of the audience. The spectator felt less temptation to identify the actor with his role. Since 1700, the art of acting has declined due to, first, the infiltration of unaesthetic motives and second, the unfashionableness of improvisation. Nothing could be more decadent than a society like the present where actresses aspire to marry dukes or counts. A strong effort should be put forth to make acting hereditary and to keep those who practice it apart, trained from childhood like acrobats. The intactness of a strict convention such as that of classical drama in France makes for good acting because the rules are clear and the requirements rigid. Above all an actor should not want to escape from his own world nor allow himself to be used as a type. When actors could scarcely be distinguished from vagabonds, as in sixteenth-century England, things were better, the art became everything. Because of lack of detachment women do not make good actors; they can act only themselves.

Griffin: How does an actor best fulfill his function?

Auden: By expressing an essence other than his. For this he must have: great understanding, a double self, elegance. I mean elegance in the broad sense, i.e. a knowledge of style. What kept Narcissus from becoming a great actor was lack of objectivity; all the rest fits in: seriousness, rejection, self-love. In the dramatic situation the essence acted is not anxious. In real life the human being starts out with existence and acts to a certain extent; his acted self remains a possibility. That is, he must make a compromise. What lies in back of the actor's deed? Definite thoughts and emotions, whereas in the ordinary world motives usually remain veiled. In order to round out the play the actor must choose between two alternatives but the human being caught in life pursues a course that evades the necessity for making choices. To most of us, living has the air of a Russian expressionist play the third act of which has been lost. With great determination human beings contrive to make their surroundings sufficiently exciting so that they are kept in a state of passion which dictates what they will do next.

Griffin: What I admire most in an actor is the perfection of external action, the stage movement.

Auden: Most men think they want to live in the moment but unable to bear the consequences they go to a theater instead. For this medium gives them illusion without involvement.—Have you read Sacheverell Sitwell's

Autobiographical Fantasia? He devotes a chapter to a description of four comedians at lunch. Above all what impresses him is the appalling quickness with which they open a cigarette case and strike a match, their éclat, their "snappiness of finish."

Griffin: Yvette Guilbert—I saw her in *Les Deux Orphelines*—seemed to me a great actress. She had learned to convey many different meanings by the rare gesture, by almost imperceptible movements of the eyelid or a flashing or half-flashing of the eye.

Auden: For an actor nothing could be more important than the control of physiognomy. Yvette Guilbert's face was made for visual effects. Because of a certain grotesquerie it lent itself to caricature. It's too bad she did not do many films. . . . Unfortunately caricature tries to freeze a face, to mummify expression, to make that which is changing historically static. A good caricature—one by Beerbohm, say, or Daumier—is a wonderfully sane therapeutic thing. A fine caricaturist can visualize the complications of a lifetime with a few strokes of his pen and sum up a social truth in a way that saves us reading columns of print. From the middle of the sixteenth century caricature has had a world influence, but during the 1900s it lost its vigor; potentially good artists have been swallowed up by advertising. . . . In passing, I'd like to draw your attention to a truth that lies in back of a stereotype. Whenever a highbrow is caricatured he is pictured wearing spectacles. When one reflects one can glimpse behind this a legitimate psychosomatic observation. A man whose true world opens inward tends to develop a voluntary blindness toward outward things. Some day a great book will be written on physiognomy. Now that we can record the instant by photography, catching the most evanescent glance, subjects like phrenology, face-reading, chiromancy and metoposcopy may perhaps become more scientific or if not scientific more fully documented.

Griffin: It would require immense research.

Auden: Oh yes, one would have to go through thousands of photographs of heads, hands, bodies. If you want to find out if a person's crooked or not, don't look in the face. That is on the defensive, under conscious control. But look at the back of his head. Or look at his hands.

Griffin: Perhaps word-origins might give us an insight into physiognomy. Take the verb "to face" in the sense of to resist or oppose. For the source of this shift in meaning we must go back to the physical circumstance of rout in war. We can see the rationale of this: in retreat one's face is hidden from the enemy, whereas if one remains to fight, one confronts him. Each part of the anatomy has metaphoric application. Take the phrases "to hand someone a line," "to stomach an insult." The latter implies a psychosomatic reaction. Anger may cause in some people a disturbance in the belly, in others a flattening of the ears or a constriction of the face. Such expressions may take us back to odd medical hypotheses. The use of the word "nerve" as "audacity" was due to a physiognomical error. The nouns "lip" and "cheek" have come to stand metonymically for impudent speech; this was caused by a visual effect.

Auden: Emotions can be projected even from the lines of one's back—as any good actor knows.

Griffin: Apparently Shakespeare had little faith in the physical betrayal of character. He makes Duncan say "there's no art / To find the mind's construction in the face."

Auden: He puts those words in the king's mouth because Duncan was a weak person with no foresight. Blind to those around him, he lacked insight into the character of Cawdor and saw no danger in elevating the ambitious Macbeth to thaneship. He was anything but a physiognomist.

Griffin: To what degree can a physiognomist make generalizations about facial structure?

Auden: The eye should take in the over-all, the posture, the *gestalt* of a person. If one watches carefully one can discern whether someone is dishonorable. True, willful blindness may intervene for physical reasons. . . . But when one thinks back, one finds no cause for surprise; one should have foreseen the crookedness. The trick is always to continue the observation. One is surprised only when people act a little better than they need have. Of course the matter of age enters into this.

Griffin: You mean that in youth duplicity may be concealed by superficial glitter?

Auden: Yes. After thirty the face exposes, bit by bit, what lies behind it, the flesh being as it were a kind of negative and on that surface you see the fears, disappointments, spiritual powers coming out. Sin shows itself in the face. Guilt and history are revealed in the body; not only in the form of physical scars but in texture, bone formations, skin marks. Eckermann says that Goethe's body in death had a godlike youth about it. The same thing was claimed of Katherine of Bologna and Hector—that their unembalmed bodies long after death continued to exhale a scent of sweetness. Psychosomatic reasons may exist for such phenomena.

Griffin: If examined closely, the naked body becomes a symbol of life.

Auden: Medieval writers tried to find moral reasons why the pagans depicted love as a naked boy. They came to the conclusion that Eros deprives men not only of their judgment and possessions but also of their garments.

Griffin: I've often thought that many situations could be simplified if persons wore no clothes.

Auden: Some could be simplified; some could be complicated.

Griffin: To children clothes seem arch-encumbrances—one of those irrational, thought-up, adult conventions like tea parties, newspapers and flattery that have no real meaning. . . . When I was very young I stood with my uncle, once, in a doorway waiting for a shower to stop. Involuntarily I remarked, "I *like* the rain." My uncle sniffed, "Oh yes, I like the rain, but only if I'm dressed for it." This struck me as an astonishing statement.

Auden: Baudelaire, for instance, regarded clothes as an extension of his real self. Ideally clothes should be that. I think a truly honest person would never wear a hat.

Griffin: Why?

Auden: Except in Artic weather a hat serves no purpose. The miter, the Easter bonnet, the helmet—they function as insignia of power.

Griffin: Clothes symbolize highly personal states. Strong reasons existed why Gautier had to wear a Spanish cloak and Baudelaire a red tie. And nakedness can, I believe, teach one spiritual lessons. When I went for my army physical I stripped like everyone else and stood for a long time in line, waiting. Cold, hopeless. I felt finally like everyone else. We were all reduced to the lowest common denominator. One's personal history—whether one had gone to Harvard or committed a crime or designed a bridge—did not matter. One had become a natural person without the power of reflection. One could hardly manage to respond to the inquiries of the psychiatrist. It may not have been by chance that the draftee was nude during this interview, for that allowed the analyst to draw deductions from such phenomena as affective coloring, rigidity and posture. I felt my body as a betrayal of my self. In a nude collectivity I am always overcome by a sense of despair and non-being. Since then I have tried to determine why that artist, Abner Dean, chooses to portray his victims naked. It is, I think, because the nude person is visualized as a lost consciousness surrounded by deserts of solitude and darkness.

Auden: Laura Riding has a poem ["Because of Clothes"] that bears on this question. It begins with the line: "Without dressmakers to connect the goodwill of the body." I suggest that you read it. Her contention seems to be that the flesh like all instruments is neutral, and evil arises from the mind. She claims that clothes quench the body, "turn the gloom inward" and that, being psychophysical in nature, man must make some balance between outer and inner life. She thinks that civilization with its garments, social tabus, traffic zones, etc. is busy working out this balance. "The union of matter with mind / by the method of raiment / destroys not our nakedness / nor muffles the bell of thought."—"Inner is the glow of knowledge and outer is the gloom of appearance." Never forget that the three crises of living occur with little or no clothes: birth, love and death. The beginning, the center and the end make the individual more honest. Eyewitnesses of battle remark on how efficiently the impact of the great new bombs strip the body. If we cannot understand what we are in other ways, at least these disasters drive the lesson home. And with equal directness war and love release the essential "glow," "the shaded breast," the bare limbs.

Griffin: Socrates states—if I remember correctly—that he found it possible to fall in love with the person of a stranger, to love *at sight* with no knowledge of the character of the beloved.

Auden: Do you think that surprising?... Standards in regard to beauty vary extremely not only in different cultures but at various times within the same culture. I think a person must accept the confirmation of others as to whether he is handsome or ugly. If good-looking, he should regard this as a worldly gift like birth, money or brains: the result of luck, a fact not creditable to himself. The temporality of beauty—this distinguishes it from other gifts. It wears less well than a talent for engineering or a musical ear or wit.

Griffin: Fatality seems to attend great good looks.

Auden: Yes—not only intuition but experience confirms that. One can find a number of reasons: envy, the commonness of physical desire. Laura Riding's poem demonstrates pretty well, I think, the curious psychophysical nature of man. Dress as a symbol of this ambivalence is at least as old as the Bible where the fig-leaf aprons become the image of sexual enmity. Since sexual love has a double nature of matter and spirit, that makes it ideally representative of our human condition. Any description of sex must be pornographic. From the outside—say, to a child—there is no matter of individuals being involved.

Griffin: This shutting-off from the child of a whole world was a subject that fascinated James—

Auden: To a child sexual experience will usually seem comic. Whereas an adult knows that the individual, the spirit, the lonely I is involved. If sex were just like eating, say, it would be farcical, but you cannot write about sex without violating the experience. The factors involved are essentially changed if one becomes conscious of what goes on, therefore it is a matter impossible to discuss or explain and parents are wise who attempt no homilies on the subject—I have always found it remarkable that in poetry and romantic literature there is so much about sex and very little about food which is just as pleasurable and never lets you down; there is very little about family love; nothing about a love for mathematics which is certainly just as intense.

Griffin: To go back to the *Sonnets*, for a moment. If one analyzes them, I think they establish the possibility of loving someone whose character one distrusts. One can lust for someone one dislikes.

Auden: Yes, and this fact lies in back of the fatality you spoke of.

Griffin: As Lao-tse remarked: "A beautiful thing is not to be congratulated on its beauty. For a long time beautiful things have hindered The Way. To be more personable than the average is to invite sorrow. The kingfisher is killed for his beautiful feathers and the tiger for his skin." The Buddhists made a study of all this. They concluded that through beauty the forces of danger and trouble found an entering wedge. The proverb, "If one loves flowers let him admire the plums blooming in the snow," sums this up. He who has great looks is apt to be contemptuous of adversity and self-control and even to regard all suffering as useless.

Auden: The fleeting nature of beauty makes it moving to others—

Griffin: And more suspect—

Auden: One should take it as a momentary thing. To become preoccupied with it means a neurosis. There are people who stay always twenty inside. You look at them and think: My dear, if for one moment you'd allow your face to agree with your age!

Griffin: "*Good* looks"—the phrase itself is revealing. Because of some Platonic streak in thought, word-usage has endowed the physical with moral attributes. . . .

Auden: On some, personal beauty has a bad effect; on others, good. But the adjective in this phrase should be taken as applying to the effect on the spectator, not the possessor of beauty.

Griffin: I overvalue good looks; I give comeliness the benefit of any doubt.

Auden: One should not. As one grows older one requires in a face less prettiness or symmetry than self-determination.

Griffin: Self-determination?

Auden: Each person, I believe, has two faces—that given him and the one he is trying to become; through will he can work on the first to achieve the second. To go back to your analysis of good looks: A young face may reveal sin but perhaps not the consciousness of it. The higher the intelligent awareness of a person the greater the conflict between the lower and upper parts of his face. For a long time the ancient Greeks tended to associate handsomeness with virtue which gave them freedom and a love of proportion—

Griffin: A freedom that became license?

Auden: Yes, but Homer did not fall into this trap. When Helen appears at the Skaian gates during an interval of war, the elders pay tribute to her beauty, not her virtue

95

or beneficence. They grant she is "marvelously made" but add: *Let her go back where she came from*, not to stay to vex us and our children. In reality one can gauge a person's ethic only by his acts. The Greeks found this out. Socrates formed living proof that a man with grotesque features, although his body was strong and well-conditioned, could be the wisest and best man in the country. As a result the philosophers went off on another tangent and conceived—mistakenly—that knowledge caused goodness.

Griffin: In a number of your poems you associate handsomeness and disease—

Auden: Just to make people examine the paradox—

Griffin: It is odd that physical beauty cannot be presented except in terms of effect. And one finds very little externalization in the *Sonnets*. Many of them attempt not a phrase of description yet manage to convey a sense of the subject's beauty by the word-order and disposition of the lines. It is true Homer does not describe Helen. But in the last book he gives us a good idea of the personal power of Achilles by his effect on Priam; it is his gesture when he kills the sheep that makes Priam marvel at how goodly and god-like he is to look upon.

Auden: According to Socrates physical beauty may cause in some men memory of a divine beauty. In poets and artists the sight even of earthly beauty may bring about a noble madness.

Griffin: Sight, of course, is the most piercing of the bodily senses. When people talk in romantic terms, they refer to love at first sight—not at first hearing or first touch—

Auden: The eye is the organ of choice, the sense by which one apprehends possibility. With smell, taste, touch—all one has is the immediate data. Seeing depends on a voluntary effort. From the Bible we learn that the eye is the instrument of guilt.

Griffin: Why?

Auden: For several reasons. "Eve *saw* that the tree was

good for food and pleasant to the eye." The eye is the abettor of physical love. By means of it one can be most grossly deceived. Since the eye contains the way of gratification and refusal (the eyelid), this sense is pretty much under control of the will which makes bad use of it more reprehensible. Hearing represents the spiritual sense. Christ spread his doctrine by the spoken word, as did most prophets and leaders. One finds the ear-eye dichotomy illustrated by the conflict between John the Baptist and Salome, Socrates and Alcibiades, and Christ and Mary Magdalene.

Griffin: You mean Socrates spoke like a god and Alcibiades looked like one?

Auden: More than that. The situation embodies the endless war between external and inward beauty. You remember at the conclusion of the *Symposium* Alcibiades compares Socrates to the statuettes of Silenus sold in shops, which opened to reveal images of the gods inside.

Griffin: Sight is, then, instantaneous, positive, guilty. The eye can immediately envelop the person of a stranger. I once looked up in the encyclopedia the biologic evolution of the eye, how it started as local receptivity to light. Through generations, that developed into pigment patches growing responsive to white light, to blue, etc. And gradually the stained skin differentiated into a clear lens on the surface of a ball filled with crystalline jelly with on the back of its interior the nerve. In the human embryo the eye appears first as a line in the skin, then a fold, thence the instrument as we know it. Animals have eyes that range from just local sensibility to light to the complex, multifaceted eye of the bee. In the evolution of the senses, one can read the moral of the slowness, the patience, the upward trend of nature.

Auden: Perhaps. I am interested in the way a lost sense may be balanced by super receptivity in another area. Milton was blind. Joyce half-blind. Both evinced a greater grasp of auditory rather than visual effects. Why do you think Homer is spoken of as blind?

Griffin: To indicate symbolically that he lived above visual temptation. It is, I think, a way of saying he was proof to the seductiveness of outer beauty.

Auden: Beethoven's case is instructive. Practically all his life he was open to spirituality. Why was it necessary to deprive him of hearing?

Griffin: As a matter of fact, Beethoven was in danger of becoming merely an excellent conductor. He needed his ear trouble: it gradually turned him toward true creative work.

Auden: An interesting parallel can be drawn between the W. H.-Shakespeare and the Alcibiades-Socrates relationship.

Griffin: Except that Socrates did not try to control Alcibiades, to mold him. Alcibiades wished to be his pupil but Socrates saw in his friend an incapacity to master himself.

Auden: Yes, this situation with W. H. seems to be the one thing Shakespeare cannot be objective about. The plays as distinct from the sonnets neatly illustrate the difference between *speaking* and *speaking out*. That people have found it needful to use the tautology "speaking out" shows that speech instead of affording a medium of communication has become—largely—a device of strategy and evasion. Much conversation has fallen to the plane of the sales talk or the newspaper paragraph. On the rare times when people try to find words for what they feel, we say that they *speak out*. In the sonnets—particularly such ones as CX or CXXIX— Shakespeare speaks out, whereas in the plays he just speaks—beautifully, divinely of course. In *Macbeth* and *Hamlet* he is creating a world of language but in the *Sonnets* he desperately tries to do that which is forbidden: to create a human being. With the ardor of a Paracelsus, who incidentally was a contemporary, he mixes words as if they were chemicals that might bring forth homonculus. Evidently he has selected someone at a stage of possiblity. He wants to make an image so the person will not be a dream but rather someone he knows as he knows his own interest. He wishes the other to have a free will yet his free will is to be the same as Shakespeare's. Of course great anxiety and bad behavior result when the poet's will is crossed as it is bound to be. This type of relationship needs a lot of testing to see if the magic is working. Sonnets like the CXXXVII show us that in this case the test did not work. This poem (beginning "Thou blind fool, Love, what dost thou to mine eyes") perfectly illustrates the heart-eye dichotomy that figures in courtly-love literature.

Griffin: Oddly enough in mythology the eye symbolizes wisdom and becomes the divine emblem of Juno.

Auden: It is natural for the early Greeks to err in this way. For then a beauty, a glitter still adhered to the external world. The cult of the gymnasium made the people fit and pleasant to the eye. Hölderlin's lines "He values the best who has beheld the world / and the wise in the end shall / often turn to the beautiful" are a hangover of this old belief. The sight-wisdom association occurred by a curious shift. "Sight" meant the physical view. Then metaphorically came to be applied to judgment, intellectuality, etc. For clarity's sake it should not be. We should use the word "insight" in regard to mental questions. The Greeks tended to confuse physical with spiritual beauty. That is why they found it paradoxical that the beautiful Alcibiades should love the ugly Socrates. Along came Christianity and with it a shift in emphasis. The Gospel was "good tidings" not "good sights." One associates hearing with obedience and control; one listens to advice.

Griffin: In this connection I think of Van Eyck's *Annunciation*. One can make out no expression, no positive sign in the eyes of the Virgin. All the life of the painting centers in the uplifted hands of the seated figure and the poise of the Angel. It is a symbol of spiritual listening objectified in the slanting lines that strike the Virgin's ear.

Auden: Medieval writers emphasized the ear as the seat

of instructive spirituality. Many saints heard voices that inspired them and, at moments of crisis, told them what to do. In the ritual of confession the priest uses the sense of hearing as a spiritual guide at the same time destroying visuality. Monastic orders understand the superior temptation of sight to sound or taste. For this reason they all ordain as an article of dress a cowl or headdress to restrict sight whereas only certain severe communities forbid speech and none, of course, prohibits the particularly innocuous sense of taste.

seven

Griffin: It is curious that as Dante goes further in Hell he feels less pity.

Auden: Yes, he takes compassion on Paolo and Francesca; but none on the falsifiers. Then he gets down to those who betrayed their benefactors, who seemed to do evil gratuitously; they exist under a cover of ice—

Griffin: That is, the feelings of others cannot pierce to them—

Auden: They are isolated by what they are. Like Dostoyevsky, Dante exploits the figures of Satan and Iscariot to remind us of the reality of evil. He'd have had only scorn for the mechanistic theory that's tried to turn society into a mass of pleasure-seeking units. The modern view is: we live in a world of imperfect materiality. The perfection of technical methods helps us to progress. Almost no one believes in a *force of evil*; no one now can conceive conditions so bad economic measures cannot cope with them. The technician, the modern man, looks on natural catastrophes and moral disorders as flaws in the overall machinery of living. Individuals to him are objects to handle, things responsive to manipulative techniques. But Dante explained evil *rationally.*

Griffin: During his youth Dante must have felt he was worthy of Hell, he confesses to the sins of *lussuria* and pride.

Auden: He believed he escaped punishment by "grappling down the hair of Satan," thus coming clear on the other side. But we must not talk loosely of pity; it's a precise emotion. Because of early emotional experiences

101

Dante can feel with Paolo and Latini; he cannot with Alberigo or Bocca degli Abati.

Griffin: We don't know much of Dante's youth.

Auden: No. But he was a passionate man. Had he not been he couldn't have written the Fifth Canto. Whom does he place among those winds?—*those who subject reason to lust*. Do you remember the lines "And as their wings bear along the starlings, at the cold season, in large and crowded troop"? We talk, justly, of coldblooded sex, for habitual sex finally deadens the power of feeling. In this circle Dante places Dido, Cleopatra, Semiramis, Paris and Tristan, "those whom love had parted from our life."

Griffin: —those who loved "fit to die"—

Auden: There's hope for a man as long as he is joined to all the living. When this connection breaks up, he's doomed. Because of the sin of *lussuria*, the black storm buffets these figures and no punishment could be more subtle, self-determined and truthful.

You mentioned before that Dante confessed to the sin of *lussuria*. He must have felt—how else can we account for his sympathy with Paolo?—that under different circumstances his love for Beatrice and the lady of the window might have become a self-yielding. In sacred and profane love he recognizes an impulse that sends the spirit in one case eventually toward God, in the other toward the sexual object. This force he likens to a wind that may be savage or smooth: he describes Paolo and Francesca as being borne "*so light* upon the wind," and across the distance that separates them Dante cries: "Come speak to us, if none denies it." Then the power of the breath desiring communication works with an initiative of its own, and Dante's cry arouses in the couple their will which takes the form of a different wind driving them in the direction of knowledge and understanding. By one impulse they soar from the center of the condemned band and rise toward the place where the poets await them.

Griffin: It is a wonderful stroke that Dante causes the storm to cease during their dialogue.

Auden: The desire to communicate destroys sensuality. That long speech beginning "O living creature" occurs without being given to either Paolo or Francesca, but as if issuing from both their mouths. They say, "Of that which it pleases thee to hear and speak, we will hear and speak with you." In other words, this is no rhetorical thing. Whereas a lesser poet would have made of their words a statement, Dante creates the effect of a spiritual influence. We see that Hell has instructed them. In this passage between the quick and the dead, there is speaking, there is listening. Afterward Dante bows his face and remains silent a long while. When he speaks it is with directness and self-involvement. After he has heard Francesca's story, he loses consciousness and falls "as a dead body falls." His identification and pity force him to know their death. Sexual love becomes the destruction of *self* and its recalled image blanks out the world.

Griffin: The storm metaphor for this has been used by others, more romantically by the Marquis de Sade, for instance. A bolt of lightning kills Justine. Do you think that the element of violence exceeds pleasure or fulfillment in sex?

Auden: To know others through sex means to know them in a divisive way. We associate sex largely with youth because to the young the world has an aspect of hostility. The sexual experience is not only divisive but consolatory. Because of the melancholy that attacks young people, sex— the overwhelming discovery of it in its strength—comes to them as a reward without which there'd be nothing for them to do but commit suicide. The young lover resembles a figure in a Rouault, a thick black line separates him not only from his environment and family but even from his partner.

Griffin: When children reach adolescence parents sense the break in communication and say, what's the matter?, etc. But one cannot speak out, for about the sex-experience one can't be articulate. Even if one could, the others wouldn't recognize that description as anything they'd known because sex-experience can't be rightly remembered; what we recall remains a romanticization.

Auden: Quite. If you'll have the patience, I'd like to read you something from the *Tristan* libretto. The lovers have met by night in the garden; this is what they say:

> Art thou mine?
> Do I behold thee?
> Do I embrace thee?
> Can I believe it?
> At last! At last!
> Here on my breast!
> Do I then clasp thee!
> Is it thy own self?
> Are these thine eyes?
> These thy lips?

—etcetera, for thirty lines in the same vein. You'll call this drivel but it is also, I think, amazingly accurate. At this point, the writer frankly rejects intellectual symbols and turns to rhythm and a tomtomlike repetition to express the sexual. That many lovers are moved to try to write or speak poetry is not a good thing—it would be better for them to make love. One feels this, too, in connection with Tristan and Isolde, knowing, however, the limitations of the opera stage. In view of this, the resource to such compulsive speech provides the next best thing. When one feels, one talks beside the mark.

Griffin: Sex can never be understood *from the outside*, can it?

Auden: No. For this reason, *any* description of the sexual act must be pornographic. Becoming conscious of it essentially changes the experience and that precludes any discussion of it. To a child it will seem comic or uninteresting; the adult knows the spirit is involved.

Griffin: Along the beach at Naples at twilight I once came upon a couple having intercourse. Close by, a child was playing, collecting shells, molding shapes in the sand without concern for what the others were doing... and the lovers remained unconcerned with the child.

Auden: Yes, the nature of erotic love causes forgetfulness of the child, the figure of charity. Then, other human beings within the periphery of the lovers become accidental, unrelated to the world of feeling in which the lovers are commanded to exist. But the others cannot be called "intruders"; there's no reason why they should or shouldn't be there.

Griffin: How sharply that world of feeling separates the lover from the world.

Auden: The old stories symbolized this by an external act, perhaps by the swallowing of a love-draught. In the Tristan legend the potion acts as an excuse for loving when your duty demands that you don't. Of course, it motivates King Mark's forgiveness, too; he's more concerned with the defection of his knight than with the queen's disloyalty. The juice of the purple flower in *A Midsummer Night's Dream* intimates that love, after all, may be chemical or accidental. In many fairy tales the cockadoodle-broth preceding love indicates that the condition of being in love is a toxic state. Though we believe our love to be caused by the innate value of an object, we must beware for the sake of the object which may need quite different things; we must beware for our own sake. Notice, too, that the potion is something you always get for another, not for yourself.

Griffin: Not till Dante has gone through the circles of Purgatory does he arrive at the Garden of Eden.

Auden: And beyond that he comes to the City of God. In the eyes of the Church the City of God lay at the end of stages of Self-Change; that is, you began with the human world, with the history of damnation, and advanced, if you advanced at all, to the lost state of innocence represented by the Garden in Christian myth (by the golden age in Hesiod), and from that went on to the state of infallibility where

105

temptation itself was impossible. What Dante describes in the *Inferno* and the *Purgatorio* is the World. Here visual setting becomes the symbol of reality. He endows states of mind with the urgency of places. Despair, for instance, becomes a burning plain; repentence, a green lawn.

Dante, incidentally, didn't think of erotic love as a state to be desired. In his case, it was lucky Beatrice married someone else and died young.

Griffin: But the sympathy he feels for Paolo and Francesca, and for Latini, amounts almost to an identification.

Auden: Yes.

Griffin: Latini's punishment is often cited as an example of Dante's "fairness." It seems rather an example of his shortsightedness.

Auden: Without question Dante accepted church-doctrine on this point. Though he admired and loved the man, he has to put him in Hell. Dante firmly believed that men like Latini, Tegghiaio and Rusticucci had turned from the Face of God, were proud, self-loving, resentful. It's quite possible that Heaven will be full of people you don't like.

Griffin: And Hell crowded with wits and athletes.

Auden: Hell maintains itself, Dante says, according to Divine Power and Primal Love. The souls know why they're in Hell and can be no other place. Recognizing the need to work out their fates through unhappiness, they run toward, they embrace their punishments. If there were no demons, no Minos, no walls, still the damned souls would not leave, being the prisoners of themselves. The penalties, the obstructions, are what they have done. You recall the words of Forese, catching himself, impulsively correcting his thought: "Not once only while circling this road is our pain renewed—I say pain and ought to say solace," i.e., it is pain, is felt strictly as such. After a labyrinth of false moves and losses, you come at last to the place that you know is the place for you, unfortunately—the place where you must learn to suffer; this has no kinship to masochism.

Griffin: But even if one realizes the Damned are not being tortured against their wills and Dante cannot sympathize with them (for that would imply being in the same category), it seems that he sometimes goes too far. His treatment of Bocca, for instance—falling on his head in the ice and tearing tufts of hair from it.

Auden: Oh, Dante mightn't have been easy to get along with. Were it not for these faults his acts in the *Purgatorio* and *Paradiso* would lack meaning. What Dante gives us in *The Comedy* is a working history of his mind and heart, not an autobiography.

Griffin: It seems very important that Dante was, in the worldly sense, unsuccessful.

Auden: Yes. Being an experience one can share only with those who have known it, worldly success shuts one off from the vast majority of mankind. But Dante lived in close, though often antipathetic, relation with his contemporaries. He was engrossed in the politics of his day; he was a city man. He was highly ambitious; this too had something to do with being in the city.

Griffin: What about your relationship to the city? Do you have difficulty working here?

Auden: Not at all. My friends know when I'm working and don't bother me. The difficulty is not to keep to a schedule but to have the courage to break it. Also, if someone calls me inopportunely here, I can always lie to him and get away with it more easily than in the country where your moves are watched. Then, too, I am compulsive in my work habits. If I've an engagement at six, say, and work till 5:45 and my friend doesn't show up at the proper time, I can't go on working. Something breaks the connection; this is silly. One should be able to write under all conditions. Also, my supposedly self-regulating needs, such as hunger, do not operate by themselves, but according to the schedule. For instance: ordinarily I stop work at 5:30. At six I start getting hungry. One day a prankster set the clock back two hours and I worked till 7:30 with no trace of hunger. . . . In this apartment, you know, I'm not conscious of the city out there.

Griffin: You seem to have the curtains always drawn.

Auden: I love the city; it's where things happen. It is the norm to be alone in the city. Because the city forces you to listen to other people's conversations, you become a public citizen. Whereas a large landscape diffuses energy, in the midst of the city you can concentrate. If your work absorbs you, no power can keep you from it; others sense this and detach themselves from you. [*He glances at his watch.*]—It's time now to go to Ticcino's for a steak. We have talked past the time when my unself-regulating desires should have announced themselves.

eight

Auden: I have sometimes wondered if what really cut Wilde off from other people weren't his great success, rather than the experience in prison—

Griffin: Yes, I remember, in *De Profundis* he admits: "I grew careless of the lives of others." A very successful person, I suppose, is not particularly interested in what others are like.

Auden: Or at any rate his interest takes an oddly unsympathetic form. Worldly success resembles sex, an experience you can share only with those who have known it; it's unlike sex in its uncommonness.

Griffin: It can sometimes be curiously confused with sex. Getting to the top that way. And look how Byron confused things.

Auden: The legend of Dick Whittington, which I've always liked, is a conventional success story, a fairy tale. His alertness on every side, and listening to the message of the bells show his attentiveness to magic.

Griffin: I can understand that! Most of my life I've waited for the bells to ring, so I could turn back.

Auden: Dick Whittington is successful by the standards of the World. He becomes rich, a mayor, and marries the boss's daughter. In its own context the World is right in worshipping success. Its idea of success is so distorted, however, that it often fails to recognize it. There's only one reason why the World's judgments seem so often confirmed and that is because people accept its values.

Griffin: Is it right, thinking schematically, to set in opposition the artist and the World?

Auden: I don't know but let's look at an example. Take Wilde, for instance. During his thirties, he knew immense success. The absoluteness of his success, as he said, made him careless of the lives of others. He was a very good artist but not much of a psychologist, which is why, incidentally, he couldn't write a novel. In his ordinary transactions he didn't show much insight into people. He was continually making errors of approach. I don't sympathize with the way he handled his trial. From the first he misread Queensberry's character and passed up the chance to expose his bluff. The spelling error on the card sent to the club, the bouquet of vegetables, things like that should have given Wilde some hint of the sort of man this was. The young, rather irresponsible Robert Ross advised Oscar to see his solicitor and get a warrant for the arrest of his tormentor. When the solicitor asked his client on oath whether there was truth in the libel, Wilde assured him he was innocent. In the social world, Wilde had realized the grace of lying, and even written an essay called "The Decay of Lying." But one would have thought that even he would know this was not the correct time to lie. It appears almost as if the success of Wilde had begun to exhaust itself and that the protagonist knew he must force himself forward. Sometimes the only way a person can grow is by letting his sense of drama carry him away.

Griffin: Is it true to say Wilde was attracted by doom?

Auden: I think not. He was too much of a hedonist. The conflict between these elements creates much of the tension in *The Picture of Dorian Gray*. Of course, the hedonist places an excessive value on youth, believing as he does that the young are frank, beautiful, innocent, good. During his examination at the trial, Wilde sadly remarked: "The pleasure to me was being with those who are young, bright, happy, careless and free. I do not like the sensible and I do not like the old."

Griffin: *The Picture of Dorian Gray* might be called a youth parable.

Auden: When he wrote it, Wilde was thirty-eight. At that time he had had some but not much sexual experience outside marriage and then, no longer young, he could fully appreciate the poignance of youth, its intensity and self-absorption. The plot of the story parallels the Narcissus myth: Echo becomes the actress; the pool, the portrait. Being self-centered, the hedonist regards the external world as the reflection of a mirror; his own image as unchanging.

Griffin: The trial and prison were to teach Wilde something of the darkness of life, and that he himself could, in fact must, change. Out of these experiences came his best work: "The Ballad of Reading Gaol" and *De Profundis.*

Auden: But in what sense did he change? Morally speaking, the only way a prison experience can "decriminalize" one is by making one older. For a person like Wilde to have four close walls around him reduced his chance to choose between x and y but there can be no conventional question of "reformation." While Wilde's experience at Reading may have given him a deeper sense of the intractability of life, it could scarcely be expected to have changed his predilections. To too great an extent Wilde believed in the uniqueness and preciousness of the personality. And while it is true he said, in gaol, that henceforth he was interested only in writing about the Artistic Life in relation to Christ, we have to counterbalance this with the far different facts of his later life. Oscar liked the incense, the aesthetic aspects of the Roman Catholic faith. His friends, Robert Ross, Ada Leverson and others, arranged a party for him just after his release. Around him were smiling faces, wine, bouquets of flowers. During a short interval in the celebration, he found time to write a letter to a Roman Catholic monastery asking if he might retire there for six months, and sent it off by cab. Later, a messenger returned with a reply. His request was refused; they could not accept him on an unconsidered impulse, he must think it over for at least a year. This affected him so that he wept, but Ross, turning to him, managed to direct his thoughts toward a different aspect of the future and began to put in motion their arrangements to immediately leave for Dieppe. There are moments like this when *the edge of a person's life* is seen.

Griffin: Wilde's attitude toward religion was not simple or romantic. Do you know his remark: "I cannot stand Christians because they are never Catholics and I can't stand Catholics because they are never Christians." . . . The prison experience certainly taught him how to shudder.

Auden: Until the débâcle, and perhaps after, what Wilde valued most was what gave him pleasure. He pretty much accepted the values of the World. What does the World think of as good, as fruitful for life? What does it think of as useless? That which is good, says the World, is money, birth, beauty, brains. The useless is suffering. Suffering is negative, barren, vulgar. Oscar at his best had good looks, magnetism, wit, money, but he was dominated by the dread of ascending to a higher life. By the World's standards he was successful but this did not, in the concrete, make things easier for him. Look how his success exposed him. One of his characters in *Dorian Gray* is made to remark: "Young people nowadays imagine that money is everything." "Yes," Sir Henry Wotton says, "and when they grow older they know it." This is so revealing. Wilde, you know, adored pomp and privilege, and, though clapped in gaol, he didn't change his colors. He did not come into his power in a slow organic way so that the suffering could be integrated into his life. Somewhere in his *Autobiography*, Douglas claims that Wilde was bitter toward him after the experience, not because of anything he had done but because he, Douglas, had grown older and lost physical attractiveness.

Griffin: That's the sort of thing a person like Douglas would say. Can't you hear the tone in which he'd say it? . . . There might be some truth in the charge that Wilde at first regarded Douglas as an aesthetic object but, in prison, he realized that he'd never known the nature of his friend and their relationship had been, to a certain extent, mysterious. At the end of *De Profundis*, Wilde says "Remember, also, I have yet to know you. Perhaps we have yet to know each other. Do not be afraid of the past." After his release, Wilde met Douglas at Rouen, despite the great efforts of others to keep them apart. Loyally he seemed to preserve a warmth toward his friend up to the end. In his language Wilde used the symbol of money in odd ways. He thought emotions had to be "paid for," and that one could not appreciate the quality of an emotion "until the bill came in."

Auden: Money is a kind of touchstone. It's always significant how a writer feels about money.

Griffin: He may not feel anything, but just want it.

Auden: Yes. Many of the situations in *Dorian Gray*, for instance, since they're buried in the unconscious, are not clear. Take the Dorian Gray-Alan Campbell episode. What comes out in this part of the story is the power of the wish. For in Wilde's novel, unbelievably, the invert blackmails rather than is blackmailed. And that this type of blackmail proves successful narrowly dates the story.

Griffin: Broadly speaking, Wilde was a precursor of the existentialist hero. He was an envoy-extraordinary and a timeserver, and how bitterly he was taught the lesson of time. The future, perhaps, seemed as absurd to him as the present. The only thing he submitted to was the savage force which hurled everyone towards men and things.

Index

Other Grey Fox Books

Daniel Curzon	*Human Warmth & Other Stories*
Guy Davenport	*Herakleitos and Diogenes* *The Mimes of Herondas*
Edward Dorn	*Selected Poems*
Lawrence Ferlinghetti	*The Populist Manifestos*
Allen Ginsberg	*Composed on the Tongue* *The Gates of Wrath: Rhymed Poems* *1948–1952* *Gay Sunshine Interview* (with Allen Young)
Richard Hall	*Couplings: A Book of Stories*
Jack Kerouac	*Heaven & Other Poems*
Stanley Lombardo	*Parmenides and Empedocles*
Michael McClure	*Hymns to St. Geryon & Dark Brown*
Frank O'Hara	*Early Writing* *Poems Retrieved* *Standing Still and Walking* *in New York*
Charles Olson	*The Post Office*
Michael Rumaker	*A Day and a Night at the Baths* *My First Satyrnalia*
Gary Snyder	*He Who Hunted Birds in His Father's* *Village: Dimensions of a Haida Myth*

Gary Snyder,
  Lew Welch &
  Philip Whalen
	On Bread & Poetry